MY
beautiful
ROOM
CREATE, DECORATE & STYLE

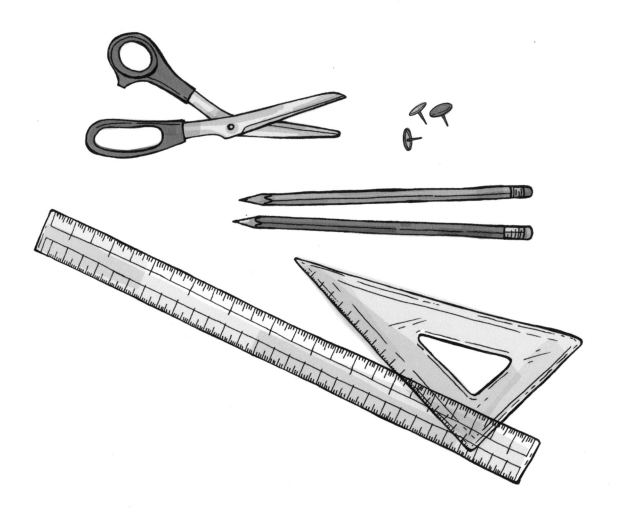

MY beautiful ROOM

CREATE, DECORATE & STYLE

Jasmine Orchard & Olivia Whitworth

Kane Miller

A DIVISION OF EDC PUBLISHING

First American Edition 2017
Kane Miller, A Division of EDC Publishing

Copyright © 2017 Quarto Publishing plc

For information contact:
Kane Miller, A Division of EDC Publishing
PO Box 470663
Tulsa, OK 74147-0663
www.kanemiller.com
www.edcpub.com
www.usbornebooksandmore.com

Library of Congress Control Number: 2016955622

Printed in China

ISBN: 978-1-61067-550-5

1 2 3 4 5 6 7 8 9 10

CONTENTS

How to Use This Book

Everyone wants to have a bedroom that looks fun and stylish and reflects their personality. But more planning and creativity is needed to design a beautiful room than you might think!

Through the great drawing, writing, coloring and model-making activities in this book, you'll learn about color palettes, design styles, arranging furniture and adding decoration and details to create a room that is both practical and stylish.

Once you're an interior design expert, cut out the walls and floor on the cover flaps of this book to construct your very own model room. Then color in, decorate, press out and stick together the models. There are stickers at the back of this book, too, which you can use to add detail to your room.

What will your dream room look like?

In this book, you'll find:

3-D room (on the cover flaps of this book)

Press-out 3-D furniture

Flat furniture to help you plan your room

Stickers for pages 38-39, and 42-43, and for your room set

Why not color in the pattern?

CHAPTER 1
First Things First

How Will You Use Your Room?

A bedroom has to be used for sleeping in, but what else might you use it for?

Would you like it to be somewhere to relax and read, to dress up, to practice dancing or playing an instrument? Do you need to study in your room?

Interior designers would usually ask their client (the person they are designing for) what they will need to do in their room. This helps the designer to plan the space and the furniture. When these things have been decided, the client can think about the color scheme, texture and style they'd like.

Somewhere to study?

Somewhere to dress up?

Somewhere to play an instrument?

Write a list of things you have to do in your bedroom and then a list of things you would like to do in your bedroom. Remember, there might not be space in your room for everything on your list. Try to stick to the essentials first.

Will it be a dressing table area for keeping jewelry and trying out hairstyles?

Or a comfy space for you and friends to chill out, where you can also read and work?

Furnishing Your Room

Thinking about how you will use your room will help you to decide on the furniture you'll need, as well as where to place it.

Use the wish list you made for your room to help you think about and plan the furniture. Remember that some furniture can have more than one use.

For example

I would like a place for my friends to stay and hang out: a bunk bed with a couch underneath could work.

Interior designers have to think about the type of furniture that matches the needs of a room the best. They must also think about the amount of space the room has, and if the furniture will fit.

For example

I need a place to study: a desk with shelves above it will be ideal. If space is limited then a stool that fits under the desk would be better than a chair.

Make sure there is enough space to pull chairs and stools in and out.

When planning the furniture for your room, you have to think about space, and how much you could fit in a room while still moving around it freely.

A piece of furniture, such as a wardrobe or bureau, desk or dressing table, needs enough space around it so that it can be opened fully, or so that chairs can be pulled in and out comfortably.

Leave enough room to be able to open wardrobe or closet doors properly.

If you like to read in bed, you'll need a bedside table with a lamp.

Leave enough space to be able to walk around the bed.

If you want a place to dress up, then a mirror close to your wardrobe and dressing table would work well.

FLOOR PLANS: The Basics

Interior designers work out where they will put
items of furniture in a room by drawing a floor plan.

A floor plan is a drawing of the shape of the floor
in a room, viewed from above.

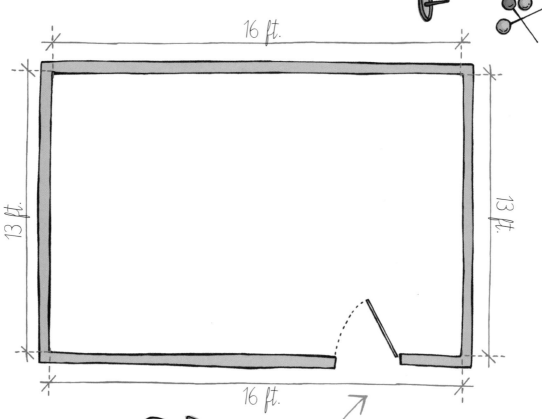

16 ft.

13 ft.

13 ft.

16 ft.

The gap is showing you where
the door is and how much
space it needs to open.

Drawing to Scale

A floor plan has to be drawn to scale.
The first step is to measure each side of
the room along the floor. In the example
above, the room measures 16 feet x 13 feet.

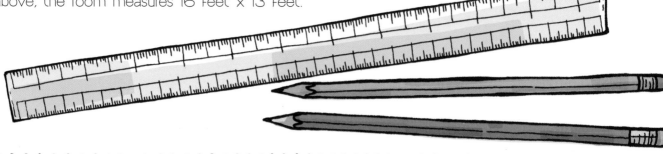

You can't actually draw 16 feet x 13 feet on paper—or the paper would be the size of your room! The second step is to reduce the "scale" and change the feet to inches to make your floor plan.

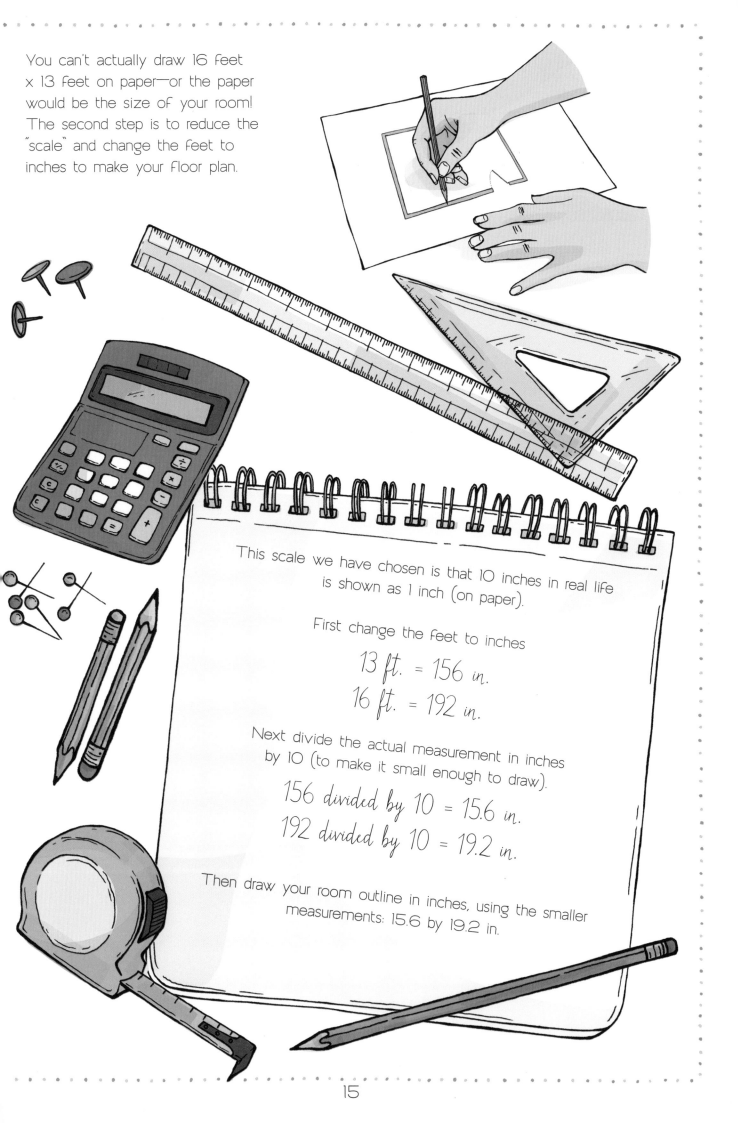

This scale we have chosen is that 10 inches in real life is shown as 1 inch (on paper).

First change the feet to inches

13 ft. = 156 in.
16 ft. = 192 in.

Next divide the actual measurement in inches by 10 (to make it small enough to draw).

156 divided by 10 = 15.6 in.
192 divided by 10 = 19.2 in.

Then draw your room outline in inches, using the smaller measurements: 15.6 by 19.2 in.

FLOOR PLANS: Adding Furniture

Once the floor plan has been drawn, the designer takes the measurements of the furniture they want to use. We used the scale of 10 inches in real life to 1 inch on paper on the previous pages. So, if a twin bed measures 75 inches in length, you would divide that by 10, and draw its length as 7.5 inches.

Twin bed viewed from above

75 in.

75 in. divided by 10 equals 7.5 in.

By drawing each item of furniture in its actual (scaled-down) size, the designer can see if all these items will fit in the room and work out the best places to put them. Everything in the floor plan has to be the same scale.

50 in. divided by 10 equals 5 in.

50 in.

A desk measures 50 inches in length. So if you divide it by 10, you would draw its length as (50 divided by 10) 5 inches. When thinking about placing a piece of furniture, you also need to think about the space that may be needed around it. For example, you need to make sure that there is enough space for your chair when you are working at your desk.

Don't forget space for the chair!

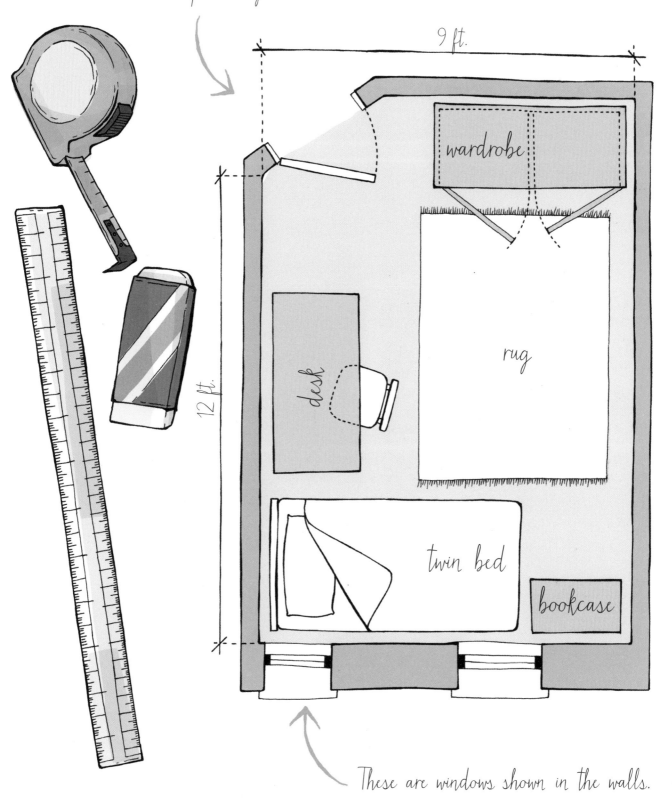

Doors are drawn open to show how much space they need.

Here's an example of a floor plan with furniture.

9 ft.

12 ft.

wardrobe

rug

desk

twin bed

bookcase

These are windows shown in the walls.

Floor plans allow designers to plan what size furniture they need.

If it's a large bedroom, a full bed, two bedside tables, a wardrobe, a desk and couch would likely fit, but in a smaller bedroom, you might discover on your floor plan that you can only fit a twin bed, one bedside table and a wardrobe.

Your Turn: Floor Plans

Now that you know what a floor plan is and why interior designers use them, create one of your own.

You can either make scaled-down drawings of the furniture you want in your room and cut them out, or you can use the furniture press-outs (on page 85). You don't need to include them all—just see what works best. When you are happy with the way you have arranged your furniture, you can stick the furniture pieces on the floor plan.

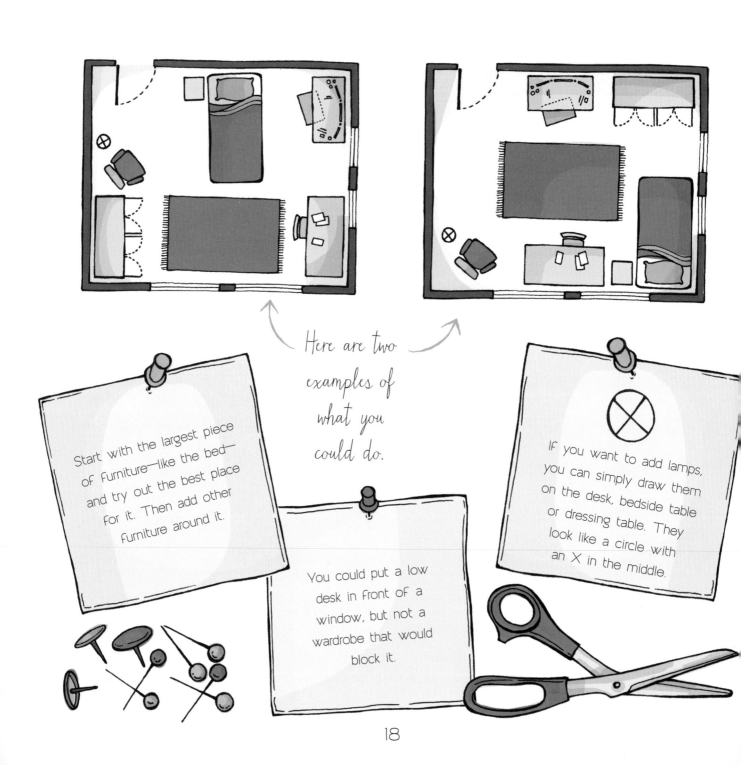

Here are two examples of what you could do.

Start with the largest piece of furniture—like the bed—and try out the best place for it. Then add other furniture around it.

You could put a low desk in front of a window, but not a wardrobe that would block it.

If you want to add lamps, you can simply draw them on the desk, bedside table or dressing table. They look like a circle with an X in the middle.

CHAPTER 2
Color, Pattern, Texture and Style

Why not color in the pattern?

COLOR:
The Basics

You probably know what colors you like, but how do you choose the colors that will work well together in a room?

Interior designers learn about color to help them decide which ones look great together, and which are the best colors to use in a particular room. By learning some of the rules of color, you can give your room a professional look.

primary
yellow

yellow-green

yellow-orange

secondary

green

orange

secondary

shade

tint

red-orange

blue-green

shade · tint

tint · shade

red

blue

tint

primary

shade

primary

blue-purple

red-purple

purple

secondary

Primary colors

are red, blue and yellow and cannot be made from any other colors.

A shade is a color mixed with black, to make it darker.

A tint is a color mixed with white, to make it lighter.

Secondary colors

are orange, green and purple and are made by mixing two primary colors together.

22

Complementary colors

are exactly opposite each other on the color wheel (for example, blue and orange, yellow and purple, red and green). When used together, both colors look very bright. If using complementary colors in interior design, it works best to use more of one color than the other, as having lots of both can be too dramatic.

Accent colors

are colors used in small amounts to add a bit of punch. Accent colors are usually bright colors. For example, a bright blue looks great with lighter shades such as gray or pale yellow.

Harmonious colors

sit next to each other on the color wheel. For example, orange, red-orange and red.

USING color

Now it's time to think about the colors that you love and those that you don't!

Certain colors can change the way you feel.

For example

Light blues and lilacs can make you feel calm...

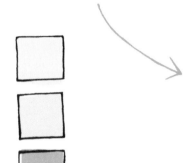

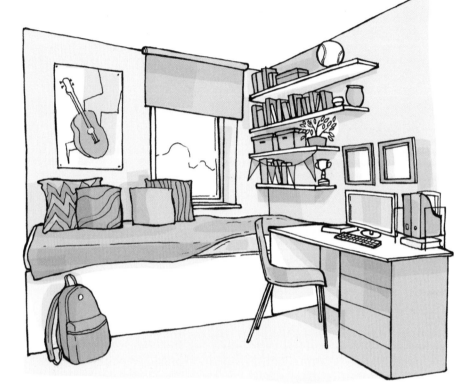

...as can shades of green. Both color schemes work well in bedrooms.

Remember

Some colors work better on clothing or accessories than on walls. Black might be your favorite color to wear, but to paint a whole room black would make it feel dark and moody.

Certain colors also work better in different rooms because of how they make you feel.

Red

is a fiery color and should be used in small amounts in a room, since it is more energizing than relaxing.

Orange

is good for dining areas or an office, but it is not calming enough for a bedroom.

Yellow

is a good accent color. It is joyful and great for a kitchen as it can make people feel hungry.

Green

can be calming or make a room feel dark, depending on the shade.

Blue

is good for bathrooms and bedrooms as it can make you feel calm and relaxed.

White

is fresh and makes rooms feel larger and brighter. It is good for any room.

Black

should only be used in small amounts in any room as it can make a room feel dark and smaller than it is.

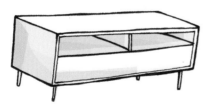

Your Turn: Using Color

Color in these rooms using the rules you learned on the previous pages.

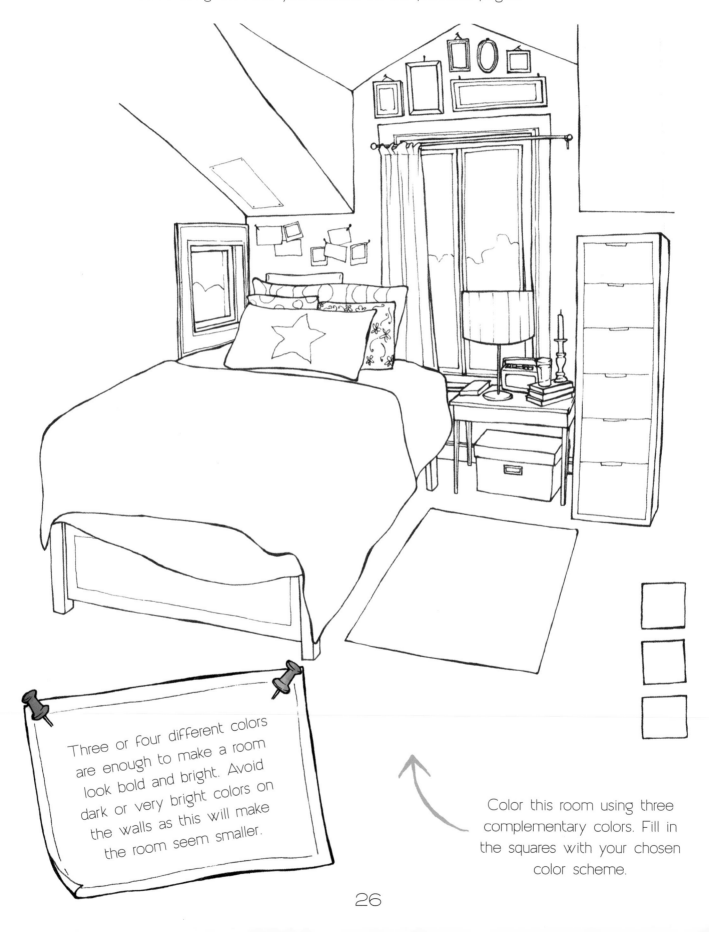

Three or four different colors are enough to make a room look bold and bright. Avoid dark or very bright colors on the walls as this will make the room seem smaller.

Color this room using three complementary colors. Fill in the squares with your chosen color scheme.

Color this room using an accent color and some lighter shades. Fill in the squares with your color scheme.

Color this room using harmonious colors. Fill in the squares with your color scheme.

27

PATTERN: The Basics

There are all kinds of different types and styles of patterns.
Most fall into these groups.

Floral and Nature

These patterns are inspired by nature,
plants and flowers.

Geometric

Repeating patterns of shapes such as
triangles, rectangles or dots are used.

Stripes

These can be made from straight
horizontal lines, vertical lines
or zigzag lines.

Pictorial

This is a repeating pattern
made up of drawn images.

28

Vintage

This term usually refers to items that are less than 100 but more than 50 years old.

For example

An Art Deco pattern is one used in art and furnishings during the period from about 1924 to 1940.

A retro pattern is a pattern that was popular in the 1950s, 1960s and 1970s.

USING pattern

Wallpaper

A wallpaper that has a busy pattern (one with a lot of color and detail), could make a room feel cluttered or too busy if it covered every wall.

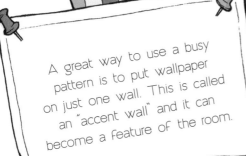

A great way to use a busy pattern is to put wallpaper on just one wall. This is called an "accent wall" and it can become a feature of the room.

Textiles

If putting a patterned paper on one wall is still too much, then you can bring pattern into a room using textiles. This can be in the form of cushions, bedding, curtains, rugs, beanbags and other fabric furnishings.

Paint

Simple patterns made using stencils or tape can be painted into a room, such as floorboards painted in different colored stripes or a geometric wall design.

Mixing Patterns

It's best to mix patterns that are similar in color or pattern. For example, floral red-and-white bedding could look good with a patterned rug of the same color. Or you could mix different colored geometric stripes on a chair and rug.

You can also mix similar patterns in different sizes, such as a large floral pattern on a rug with a small floral pattern on a lampshade.

Your Turn: Using Pattern

Add pattern to these rooms, using what you have learned on the previous pages.

Try mixing three or four different patterns from the same pattern group (see pages 28–29), or pick patterns from different groups, but use similar colors.

Add pattern to this room with an accent wall. You can add similar patterns to the cushions or bedding.

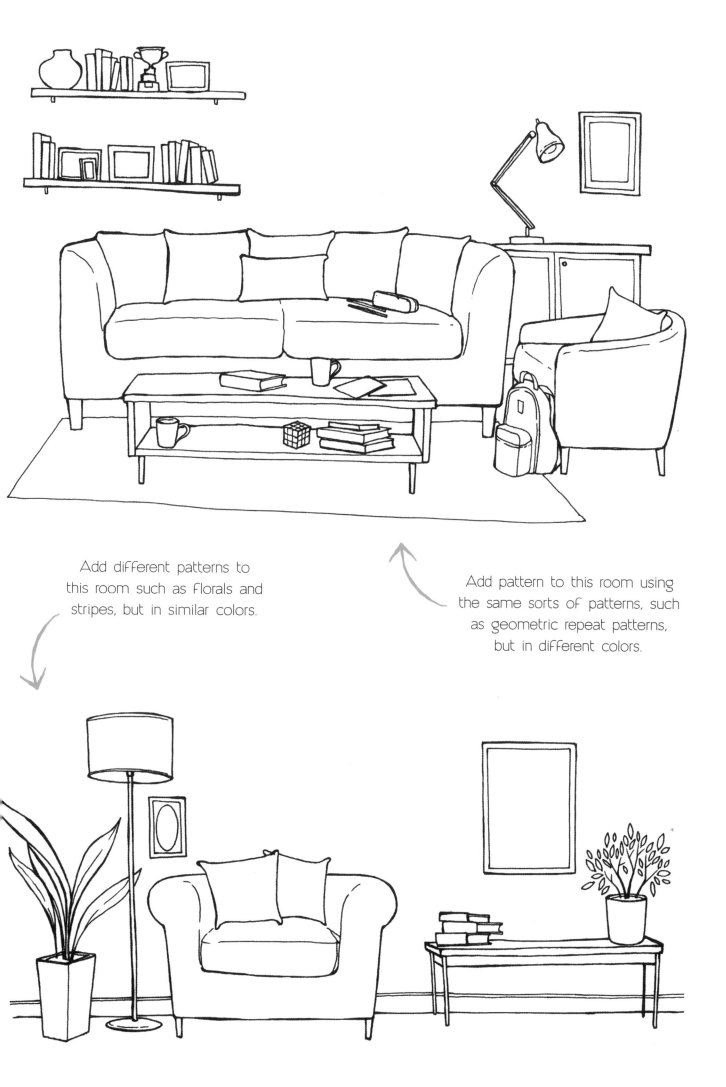

Add different patterns to this room such as florals and stripes, but in similar colors.

Add pattern to this room using the same sorts of patterns, such as geometric repeat patterns, but in different colors.

TEXTURE: The Basics

The texture of something describes the look and feel of it—for example, rough, smooth, bumpy or flat. Interior designers use texture in a room with pattern and color to create a space that both looks and feels great.

Mixing Textures

Almost everything in a room has texture, including furniture, curtains, plants, rugs, floor and walls.

There aren't exact rules for mixing textures. It is mainly about your taste. In general, try to mix items with different textures, such as a rough-textured wood cabinet with a smooth copper lamp. Or place bumpy wool cushions next to soft silky ones.

Don't add too many, but a mix is good!

Contrasting Textures

Textures that are opposites are contrasting textures. For example, you could contrast smooth hardwood floors with a thick woolen rug.

Drawing Texture

Interior designers usually draw a range of textures on a floor plan to show the effects they can bring to a room.

Here are a few drawings to get you started.

Tile

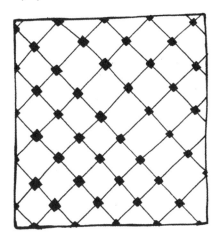  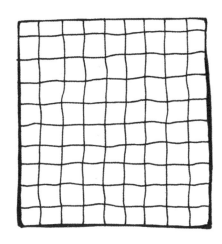

Wood

  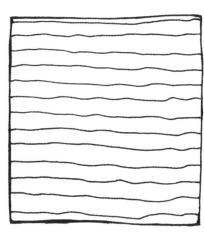

Brick

USING texture

Like color and pattern, texture can change how a room feels. If you want a very modern style, then smooth, shiny textures such as plastic and metal work well, but if you want a rustic or industrial style, then choose rougher textures such as wood and bricks.

Textiles

A good plan is to start from the floor and work upward, mixing and adding texture as you go. For example, a flat rug on top of a fluffy carpet gives contrast, while a soft blanket adds another texture to a chair. Bedspreads, blankets and cushion covers in a range of comfortable fabrics add texture to a bed.

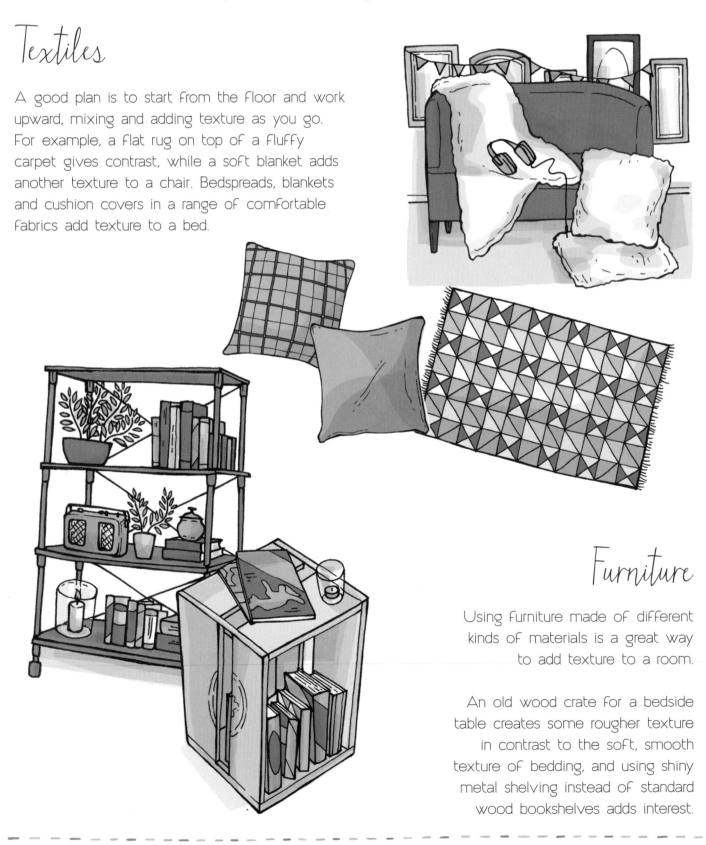

Furniture

Using furniture made of different kinds of materials is a great way to add texture to a room.

An old wood crate for a bedside table creates some rougher texture in contrast to the soft, smooth texture of bedding, and using shiny metal shelving instead of standard wood bookshelves adds interest.

Greenery

Tall or hanging plants, large leaves or flowers in a vase can also add texture to a room.

There are some amazing textural plants in nature! It's best to choose plants with colors that match your room.

Window and Wall Coverings

What goes on your wall or goes over your windows can also add texture.

Textured wallpapers, wood panels, tiles, cork and other interesting textures can go on walls. Fabric blinds, sheer curtains or velvet curtains all add texture.

Different kinds of materials add texture to a room.

Your Turn: Using Texture

Add texture to these rooms, using what you have learned on the previous pages. You can draw it on or use the stickers at the back of this book.

Try adding a brick texture to the wall and lines to show floorboards.

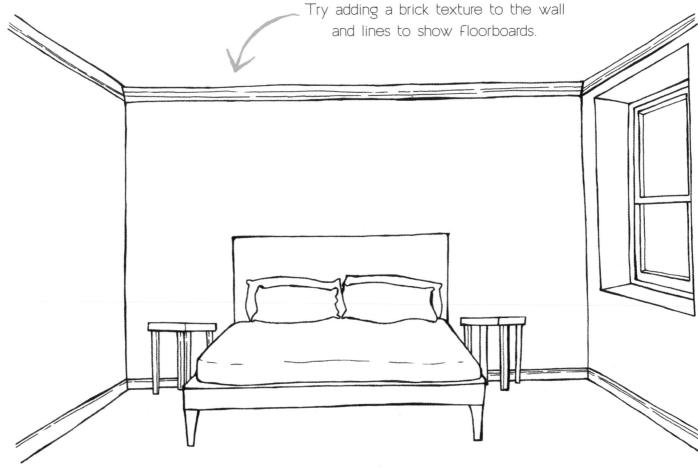

Create some different textures
in these two bedrooms by
adding headboards, plants,
curtains and cushions.

WHICH style?

When interior designers are planning a house interior or room, they will choose a particular style for their design and plan the furniture, colors, patterns and textures to match it.

Here are some of the different design styles that designers choose for people's homes.

Rustic

This style looks very natural and uses materials found in nature. Before carpets were used to cover floors, people had wood floors and used wood furniture and handmade items.

This style might include natural or painted hardwood floors, wood furniture, and crates and ladders as shelves. Ceramics, old glass bottles, hand-stitched quilts, wool blankets and sheepskin rugs can all be used.

Minimalist

The word minimal means the smallest amount needed. A minimalist room will have very little furniture and only a few objects. It requires you to be organized, tidy and to have a very small amount of stuff on show!

This style often uses plastic, metal, stone, glass or wood furniture and some good storage to keep items organized and hidden out of sight.

Retro

This style uses many items from the past (particularly from the 1960s to 1970s), usually creating a look from one particular time period.

A retro room designed with items from the 1960s or 1970s could include furniture from this time and bright colors that were popular then.

A retro style could include wood furniture made from teak (a type of wood), plastic chairs, big plants, colorful cushions, lamps and a bright painted wall or patterned wallpaper from that time.

Eclectic

This style is really a mix of different looks, old and new. In an eclectic-style room, you might mix retro furniture with a new lamp but have rustic hardwood floors and use crates as bedside tables.

Getting this style right takes more than just putting anything anywhere. It is about choosing items from different styles that look good together. It can look cluttered, and it often displays several items, such as a mix of cushions or rugs, together.

Your Turn: Using Styles

Add stickers from the back of this book to make this room look rustic and the room opposite look eclectic. You can also add items by drawing them. Think about the color scheme you'd like before you color the pictures.

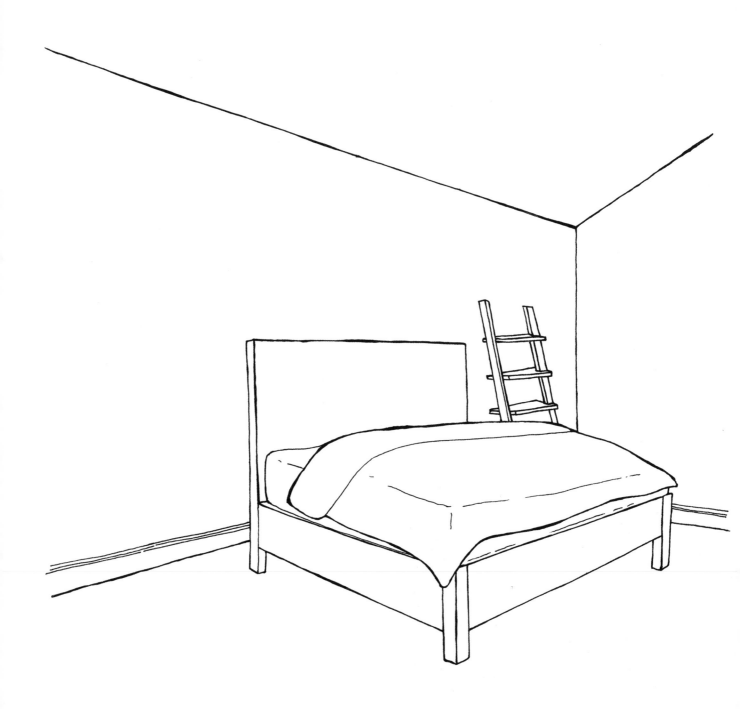

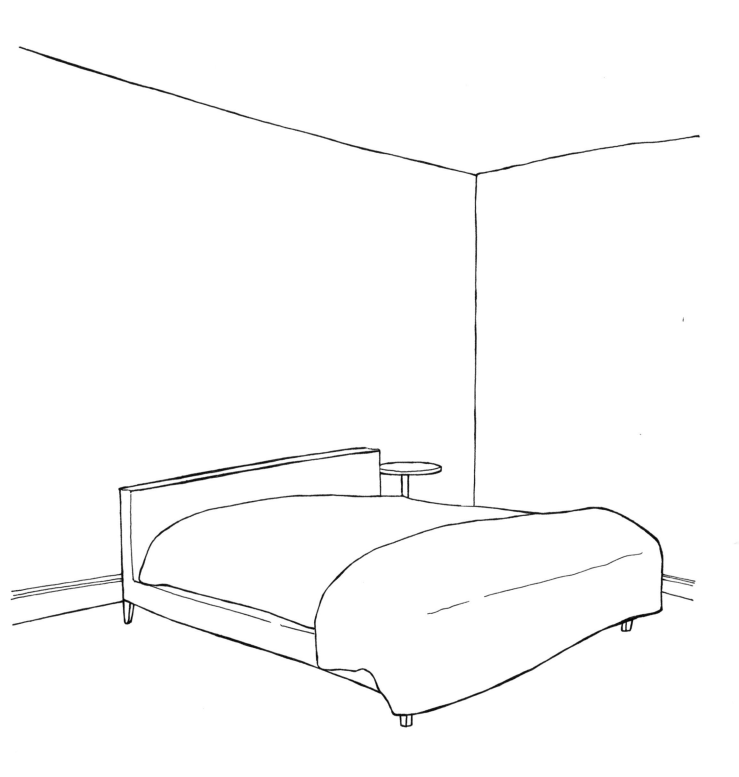

CHAPTER 3
Inspiration

Why not color in the pattern?

All About You!

Your perfect bedroom should be all about you: your style, your interests and your personality. To create a design that really sums you up, think about the things on these two pages. You will use your ideas when you create your mood board (pages 50—51).

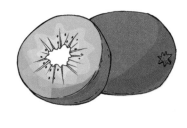

Your Favorite Colors

Choose one or two of your favorite colors, then decide which other colors will go with these.

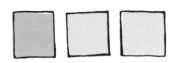

Your Personal Style

How do you like to dress? If you have an urban look, you could decorate one wall with a graffiti design.

Or, if you prefer retro fashion, why not do some research online and choose a pattern from your favorite era?

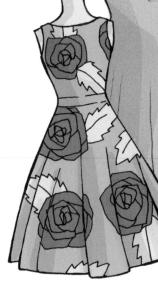

Your Hobbies and Interests

Love reading? Create a book nook with floor cushions, bookshelves and a lamp.

Keen musician? Make a feature of a music stand for your instrument—or frame your favorite album covers.

Sports fan? Decorate your room in your team's colors.

Your Favorite Things

Do you have any real-life heroes, or favorite fictional characters? They could influence your design. To create a magical theme, you could add stars on the ceiling, owl cushions and fabric drapes over your bed.

Your Favorite Places

If there is a place that really inspires you, use that as a theme. If you love being in the city, add a skyline design to your wall, decorate with multicolored string lights, metal lamps and furniture.

FINDING Inspiration

Once interior designers have decided which furniture, colors, patterns, texture and styles they would like to use to design a room, they create a mood board to show to their client. This is a collection of the colors, patterns and other influences that have inspired the design.

An interior designer will edit their mood board so that it shows all the influences that have inspired them.

An example of a mood board.

Finding Material

A good place to start looking for ideas is in magazines.

Color Samples

Collect examples of the colors you like and want to include on your mood board. Look for paint card samples in paint stores, paint a color onto a small piece of cardboard or look for colored paper scraps.

Fabric Samples

Find small pieces of fabric in the colors you like or a piece of the actual fabric that you want to use (maybe to make curtains or a cushion) or a piece of old clothing in a pattern you like. You could also ask for samples from fabric stores.

Textures

Keep an eye out for interesting items that inspire you, like a piece of wood (if you are planning to include natural wood in your room), or a fake or fabric flower (if you want flower patterns in your room).

Look for textures anywhere and everywhere—the garden, beach, garage, etc.

Your Turn:
Make a Mood Board

Use these pages to create your own mood board. Stick on things that inspire you such as pictures from magazines, postcards and greeting cards and paint samples.

desk
lamp

bureau

bookcase

wardrobe

square
lamp

side
table

round
lamp

dressing
table

stool

desk

loft bed

wall-mounted bookcase

circular side table

chest

bench

chair

armchair

standard lamp

CHAPTER 4
Your Model Room

bedside table

bed

fold-down table

MAKE Your Model Furniture

Now that you know how interior designers work, use your new skills to create your very own room, using the press-out model furniture and stickers in the book.

First

Carefully press out and make your furniture one piece at a time. Fold the furniture to see what it will look like when it is made, but don't stick it together yet. Choose the colors, patterns and style for your dream room.

Use felt pens, pencils, crayons and stickers at the back of the book to decorate your furniture and accessories. You might want to add color, texture and patterns to your walls and floor as well, so make sure you know how you want it all to look before you start!

Which colors will you use for your model furniture?

Think about what inspires you.

Remember: use complementary, accent and harmonious colors!

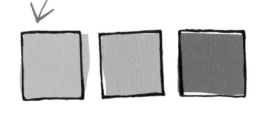

Then

Refold the furniture, stick the models together using the matching numbered tabs—for example, glue or tape the tab marked "1" to the other tab marked "1." You will find glue areas shaded in gray. Look out for extra instructions on the model pages.

Once your furniture is made, it's time to create your perfect room!

Construct Your Model Room

1. Fold out the double flaps inside the front and back covers of this book, and carefully cut out your walls, floor and support panels (the pieces look like the sections in the drawing below). Decorate the walls and floor with your chosen color scheme, patterns and style. You can use the wallpaper provided, or use the blank side to design your own.

2. Fold the dashed lines at the edges of the left and right walls, and in between the middle wall and floor.

3. Glue or tape the folded edges on the right and left walls to the back of the middle wall.

4. To support your room walls, stick one side of the right support tab behind the bottom of the right wall. Do the same for the left wall.

Try some different textures for your floor—will you have carpet or hardwood floors?

Will walls decorated with patterns or a flat color suit your style best?

Now your room is complete and ready to be filled with your unique furnishings.

Voilà!
Your dream room

Customize Your Room

There are lots of ways to customize your room. You can trace around the furniture templates to create as many sets as you like, with new colors, patterns and styles. You can use the stickers to add interesting patterns and textures to your custom-made furniture.

You can also create different wallpaper and flooring for your room—try using wrapping paper or small pictures cut from magazines as pictures, and small pieces of fabric to create floor coverings or bedding.

Tip

You could even use a cardboard box to make a whole new room!

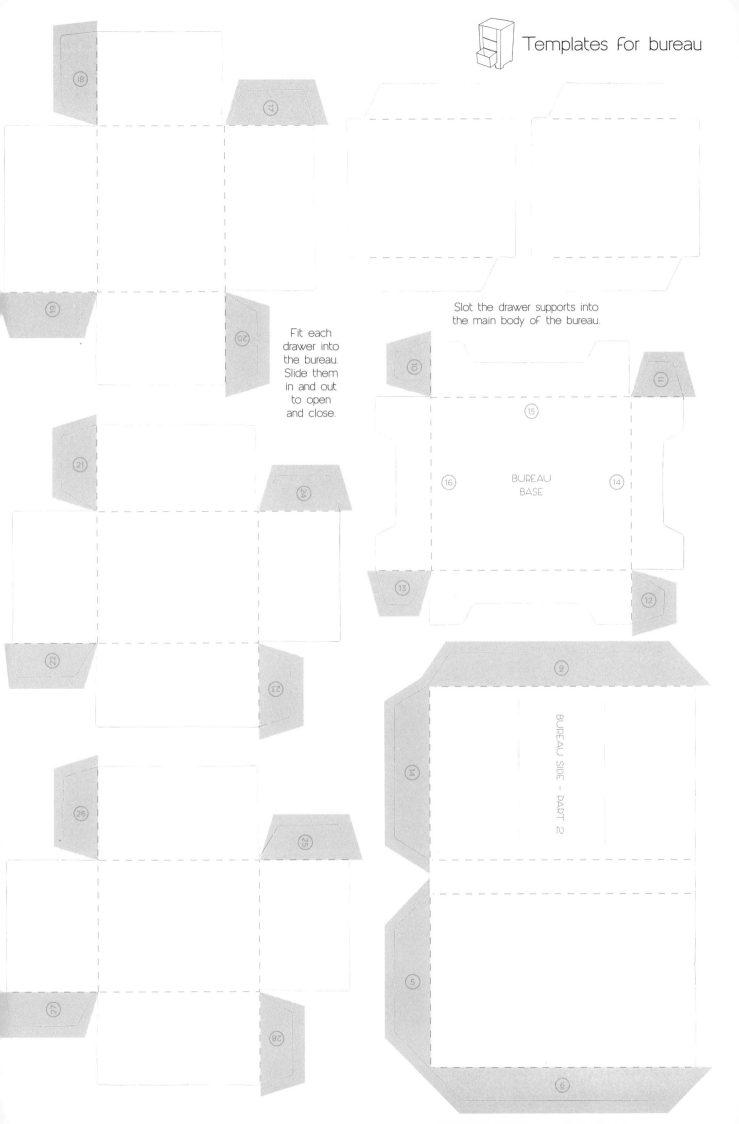

Templates for bureau

Fit each drawer into the bureau. Slide them in and out to open and close.

Slot the drawer supports into the main body of the bureau.

BUREAU BASE

BUREAU SIDE - PART 2

DRAWER SUPPORT

DRAWER SUPPORT

DRAWER

MIDDLE DRAWER

DRAWER

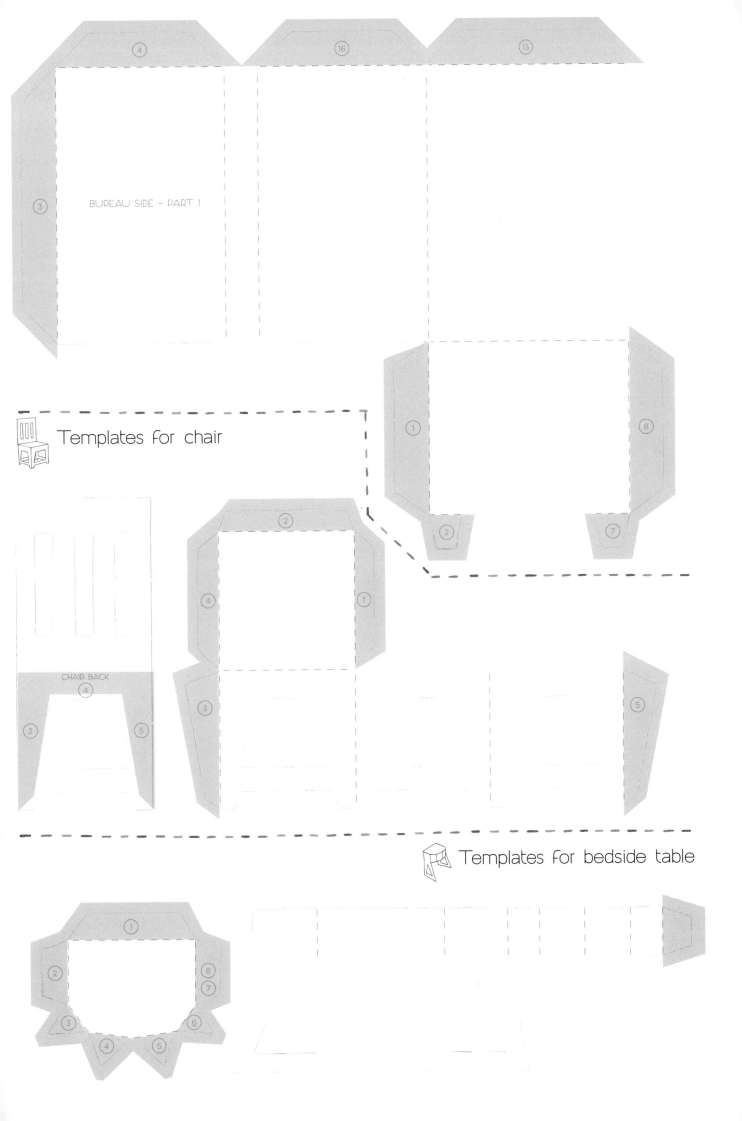

BUREAU SIDE – PART 1

Templates for chair

CHAIR BACK

Templates for bedside table

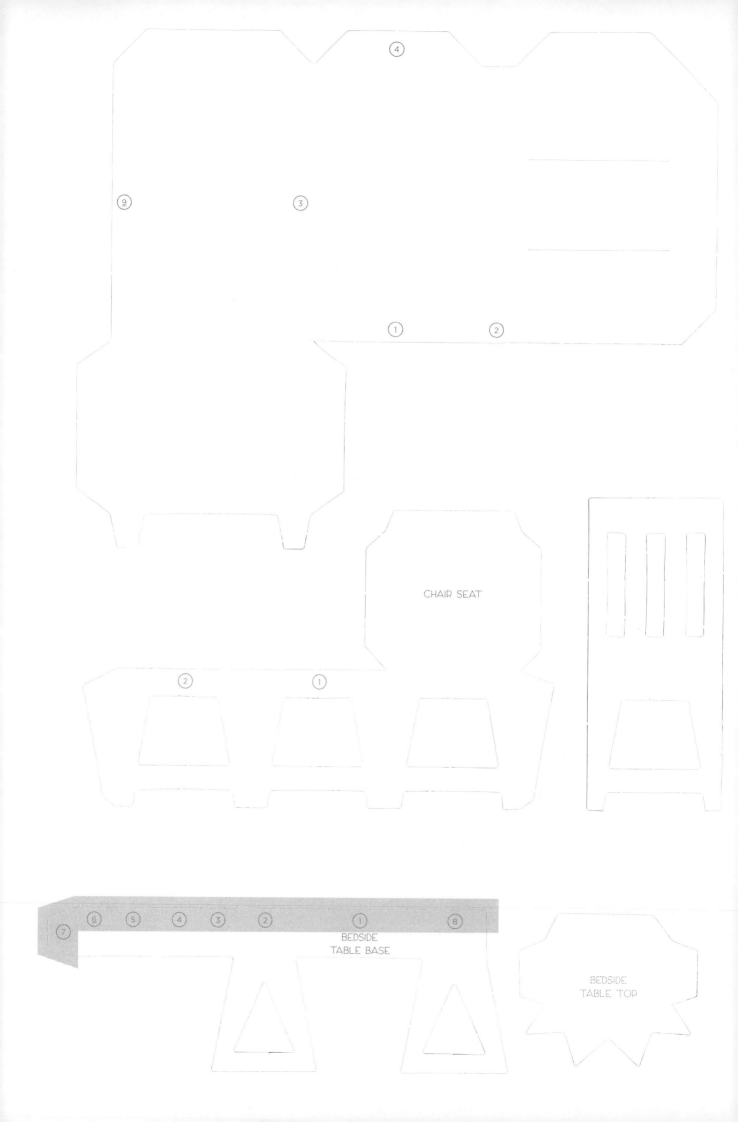

CHAIR SEAT

BEDSIDE
TABLE BASE

BEDSIDE
TABLE TOP

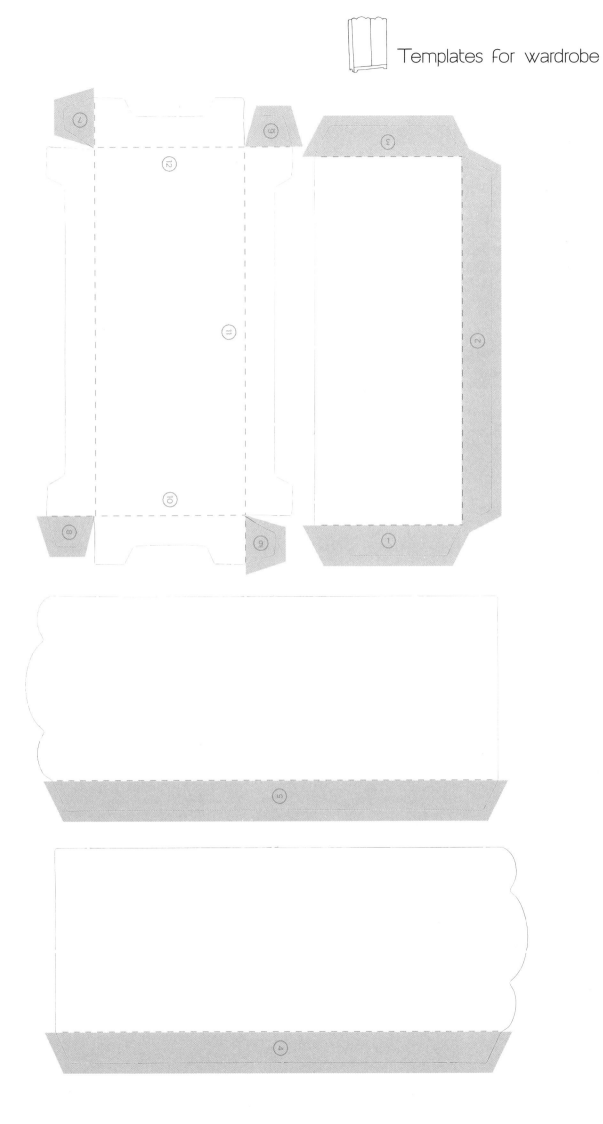

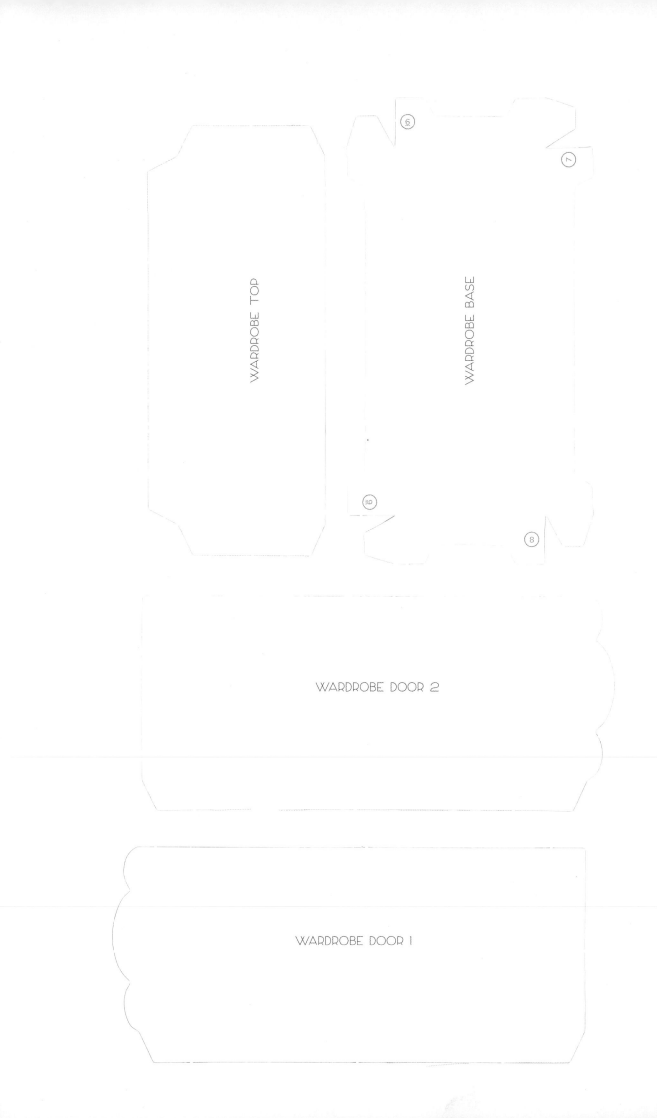

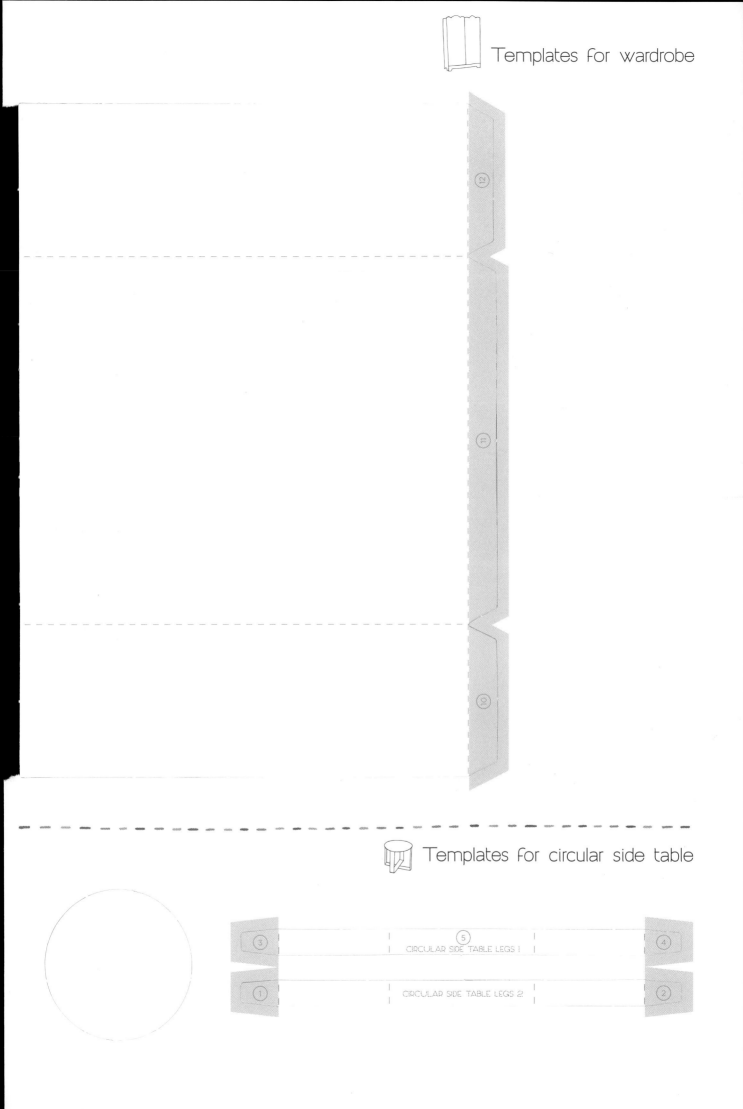

Templates for circular side table

CIRCULAR SIDE TABLE LEGS 1

CIRCULAR SIDE TABLE LEGS 2

WARDROBE BACK AND SIDES

CIRCULAR SIDE
TABLE TOP

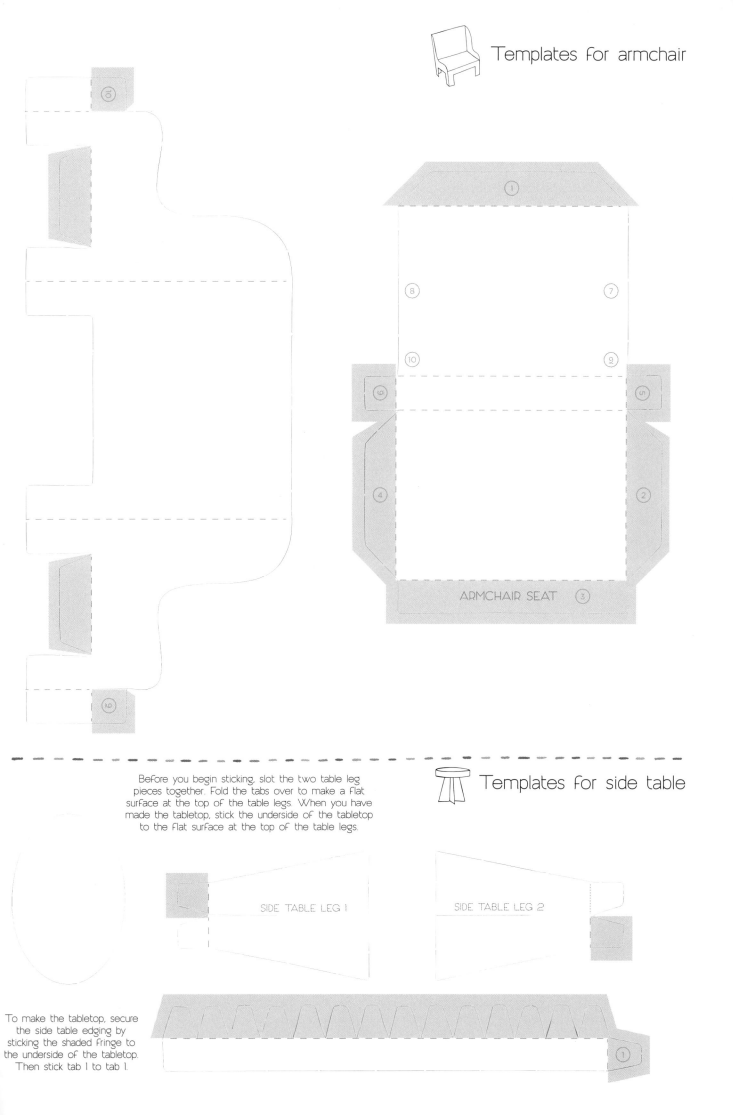

Templates for armchair

ARMCHAIR SEAT

① ② ③ ④ ⑤ ⑥ ⑦ ⑧ ⑨ ⑩

Templates for side table

Before you begin sticking, slot the two table leg pieces together. Fold the tabs over to make a flat surface at the top of the table legs. When you have made the tabletop, stick the underside of the tabletop to the flat surface at the top of the table legs.

SIDE TABLE LEG 1

SIDE TABLE LEG 2

To make the tabletop, secure the side table edging by sticking the shaded fringe to the underside of the tabletop. Then stick tab 1 to tab 1.

①

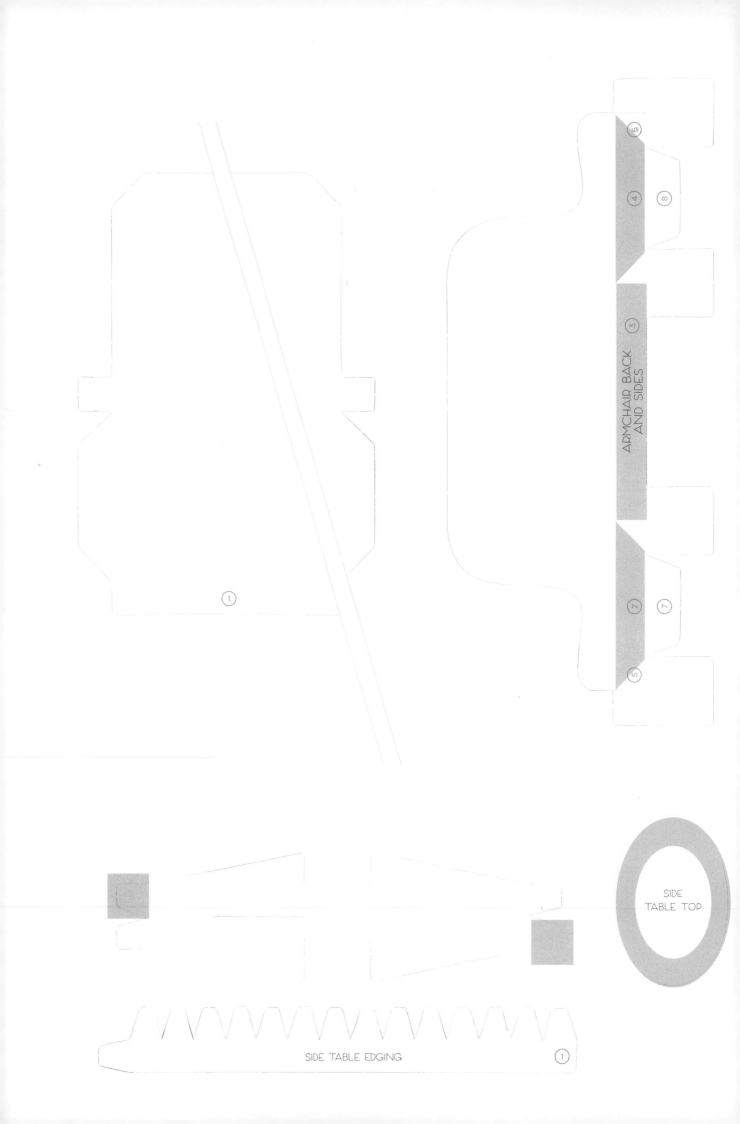

ARMCHAIR BACK
AND SIDES

SIDE
TABLE TOP

SIDE TABLE EDGING

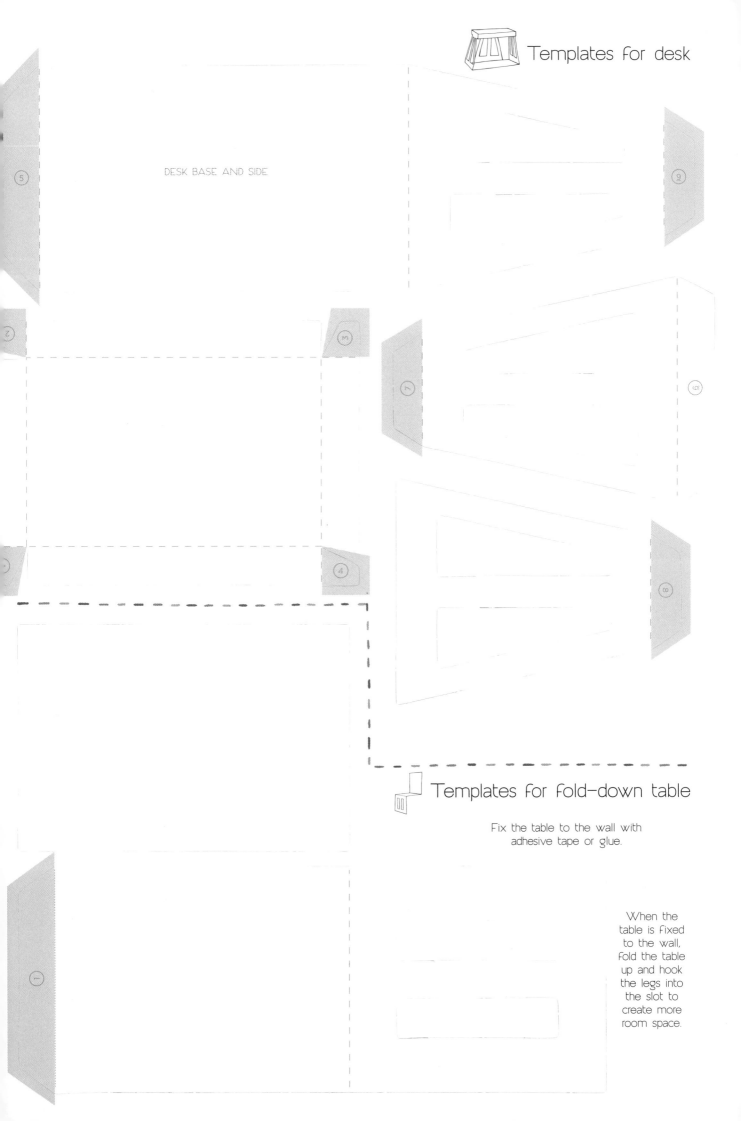

Templates for desk

DESK BASE AND SIDE

Templates for fold-down table

Fix the table to the wall with adhesive tape or glue.

When the table is fixed to the wall, fold the table up and hook the legs into the slot to create more room space.

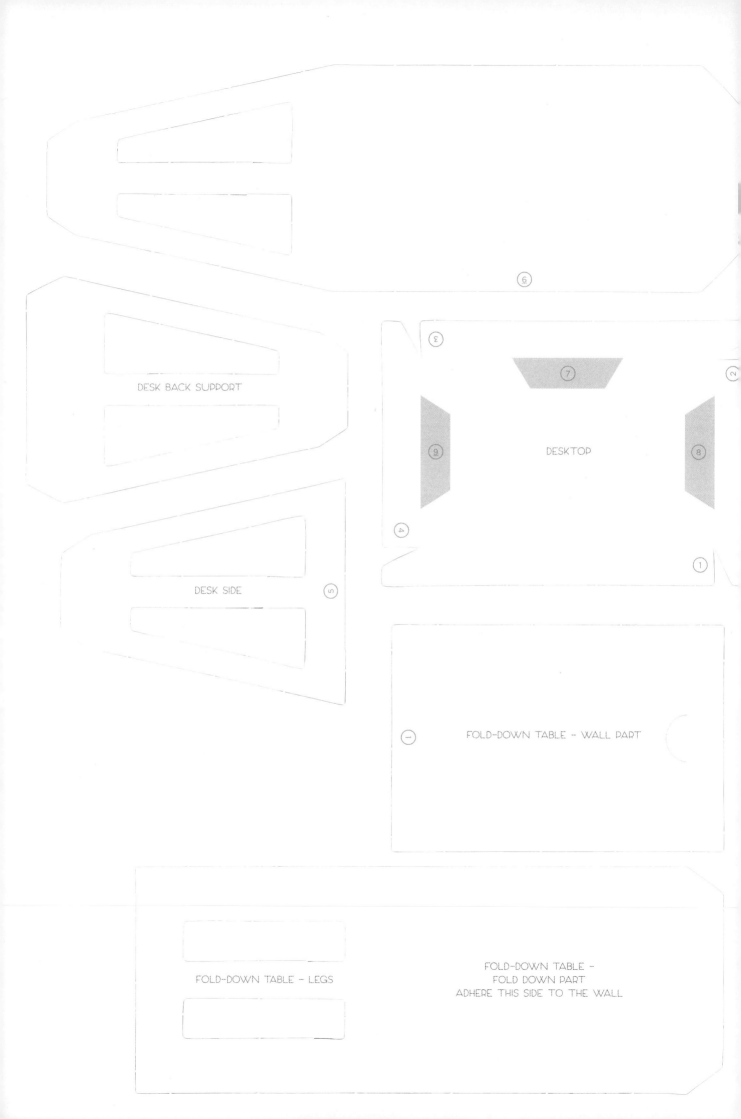

DESK BACK SUPPORT

DESK SIDE

⑥

③

⑦

②

⑨ DESKTOP ⑧

④

①

① FOLD-DOWN TABLE - WALL PART

⑤

FOLD-DOWN TABLE - LEGS

FOLD-DOWN TABLE -
FOLD DOWN PART
ADHERE THIS SIDE TO THE WALL

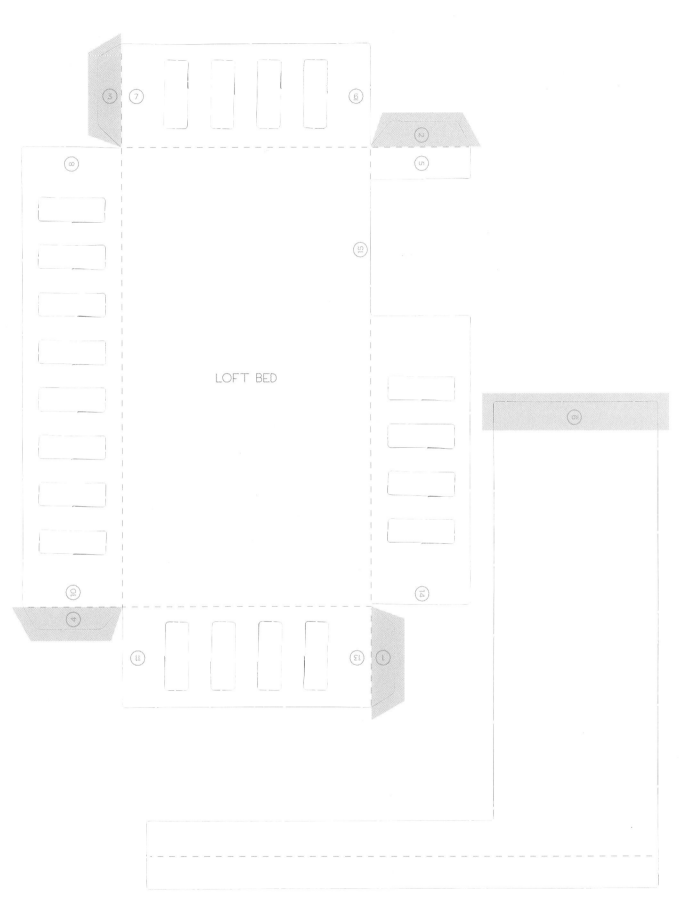

LOFT BED

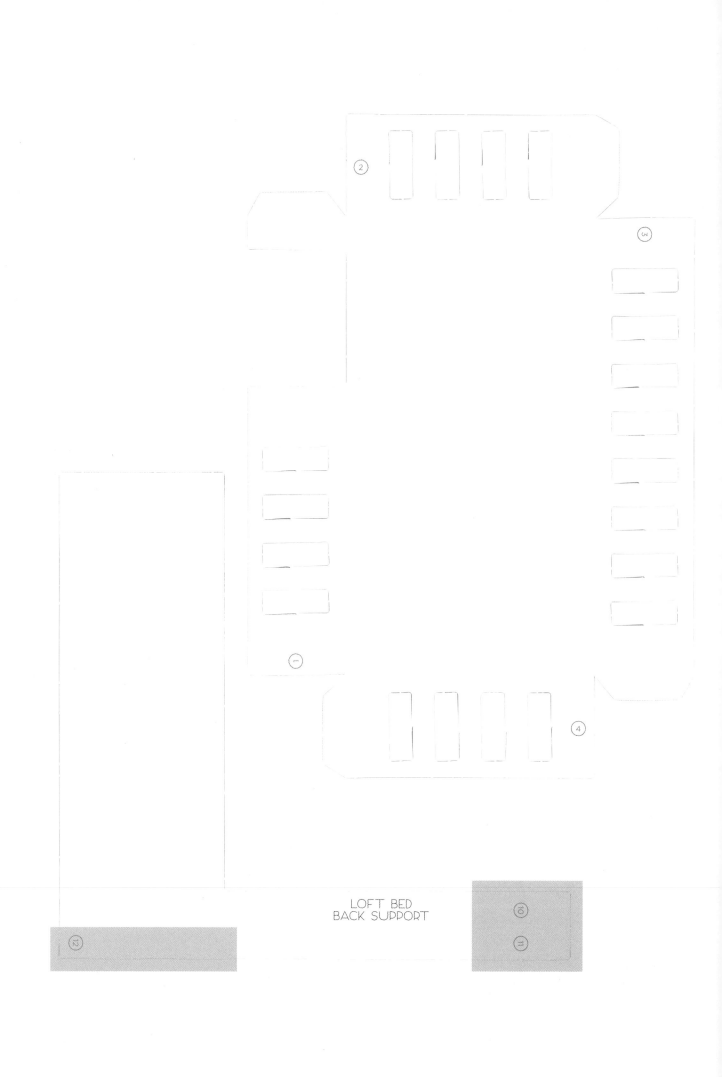

LOFT BED
BACK SUPPORT

16 15 17

12

Once you have made the lamp shade (sticking tab 1 to tab 1), stick the two sides of the lamp stand together (sticking tab 2 to tab 2). Leave the tabs at the end unstuck. Then insert tabs 3 and 4 into the lamp shade and gently pull apart to secure the matching tabs.

Templates for desk lamp

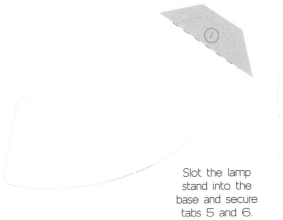

1

Slot the lamp stand into the base and secure tabs 5 and 6.

DESK LAMP STAND 1
2

3

2
DESK LAMP STAND 2

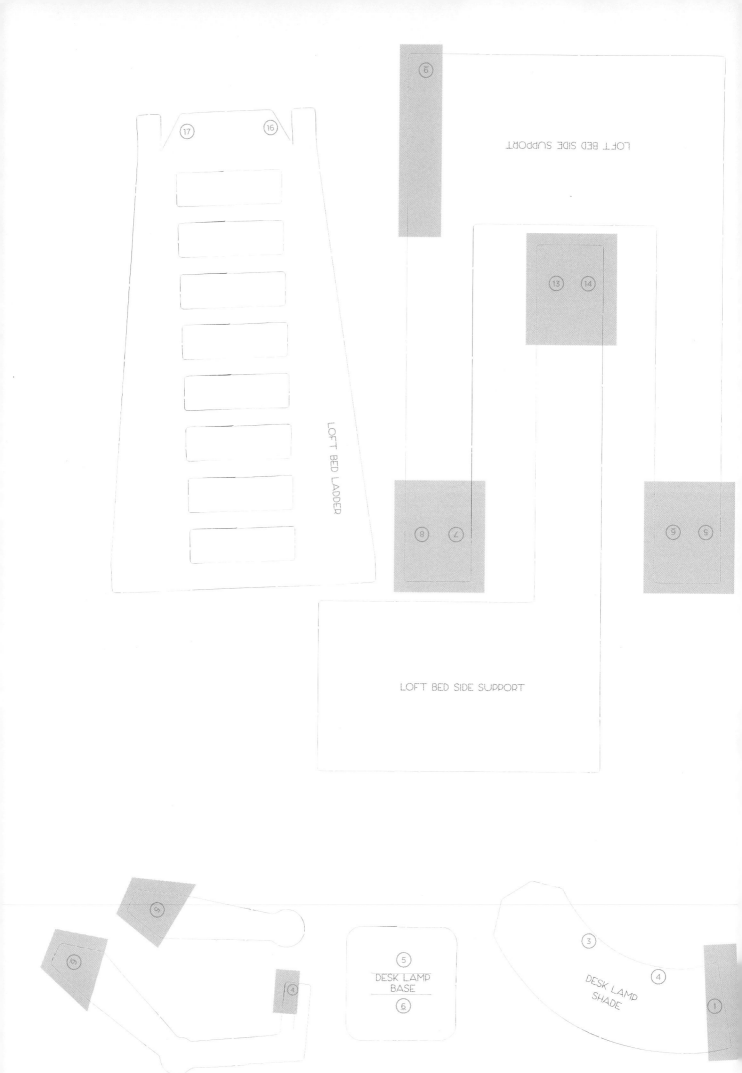

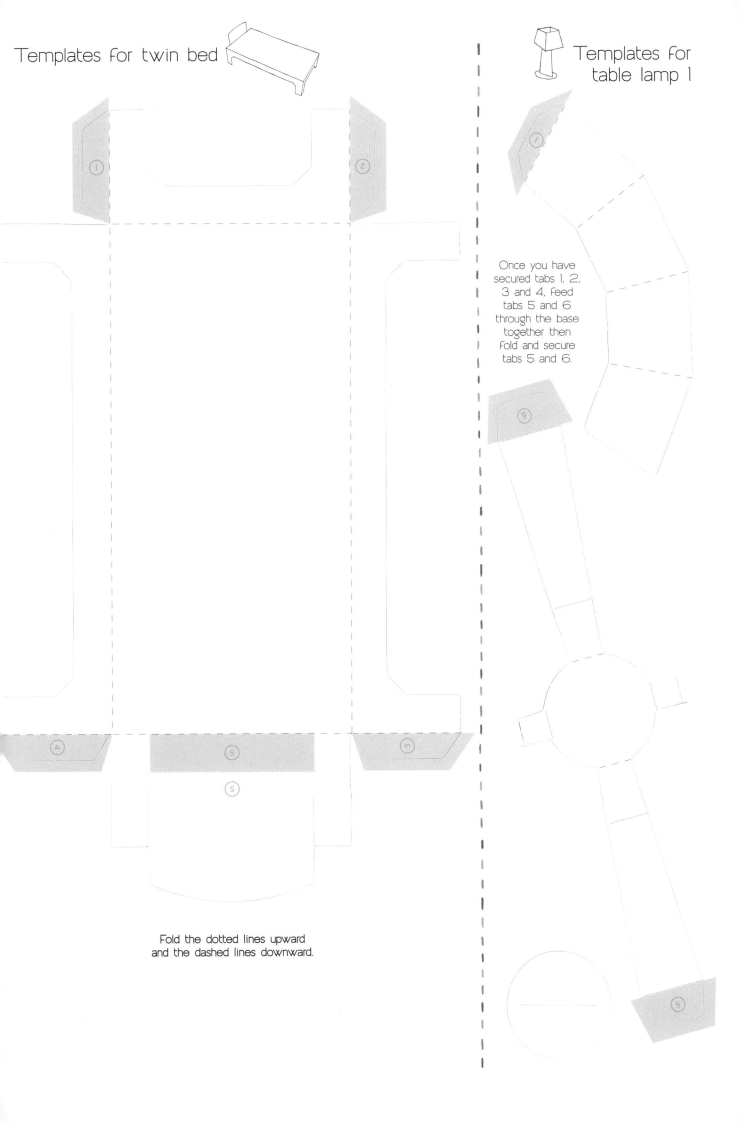

Templates for twin bed

Templates for table lamp 1

Once you have secured tabs 1, 2, 3 and 4, feed tabs 5 and 6 through the base together then fold and secure tabs 5 and 6.

Fold the dotted lines upward and the dashed lines downward.

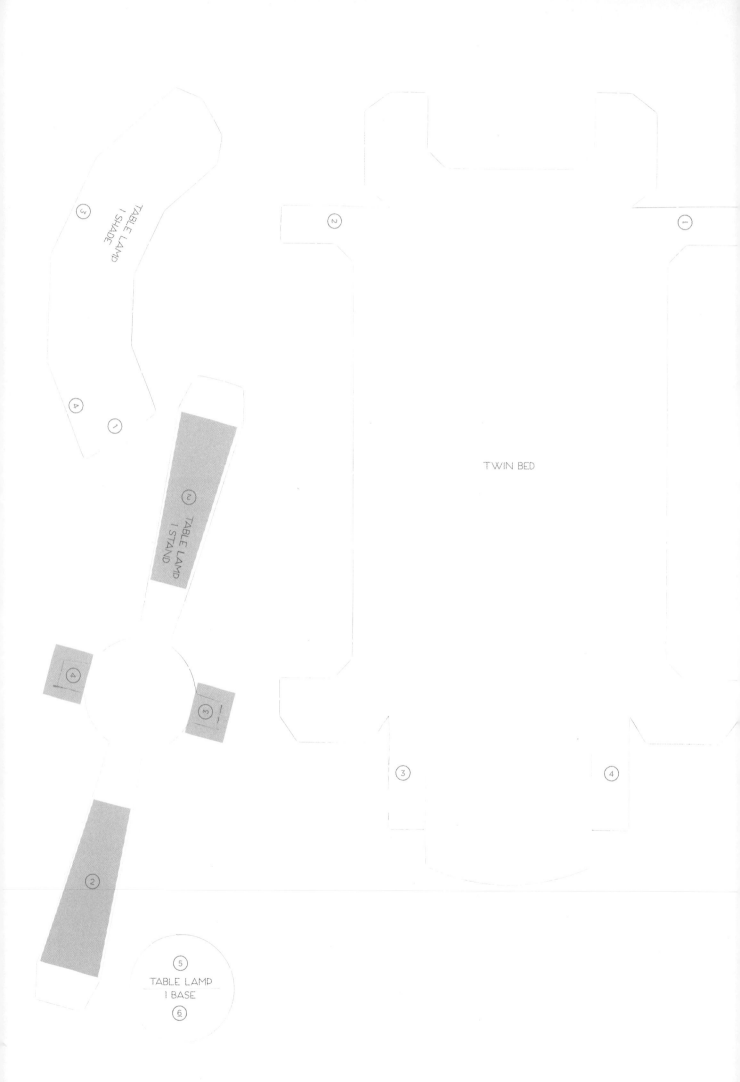

Templates for wall-mounted bookshelf

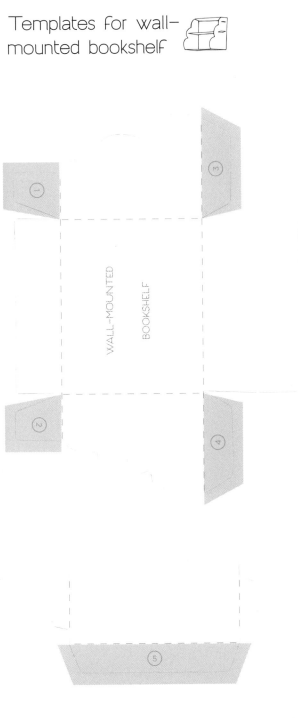

WALL-MOUNTED

BOOKSHELF

Slot the middle shelf into the bookshelf. Secure it by sticking tab 5 to tab 5.

Templates for standard lamp

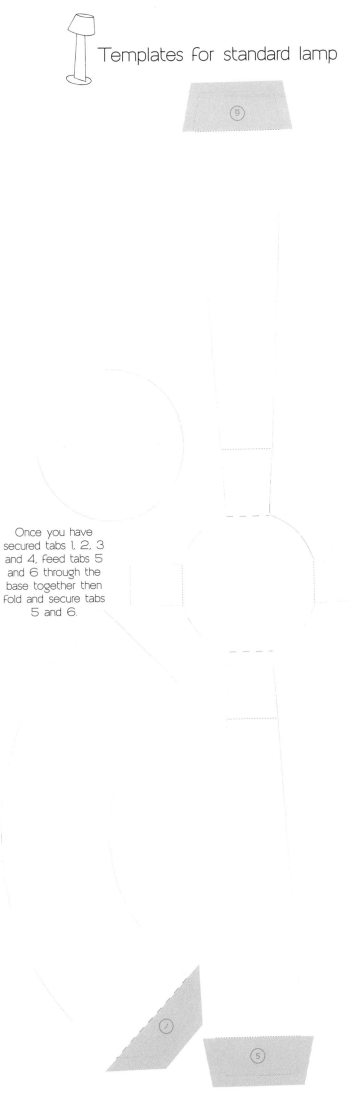

Once you have secured tabs 1, 2, 3 and 4, feed tabs 5 and 6 through the base together then fold and secure tabs 5 and 6.

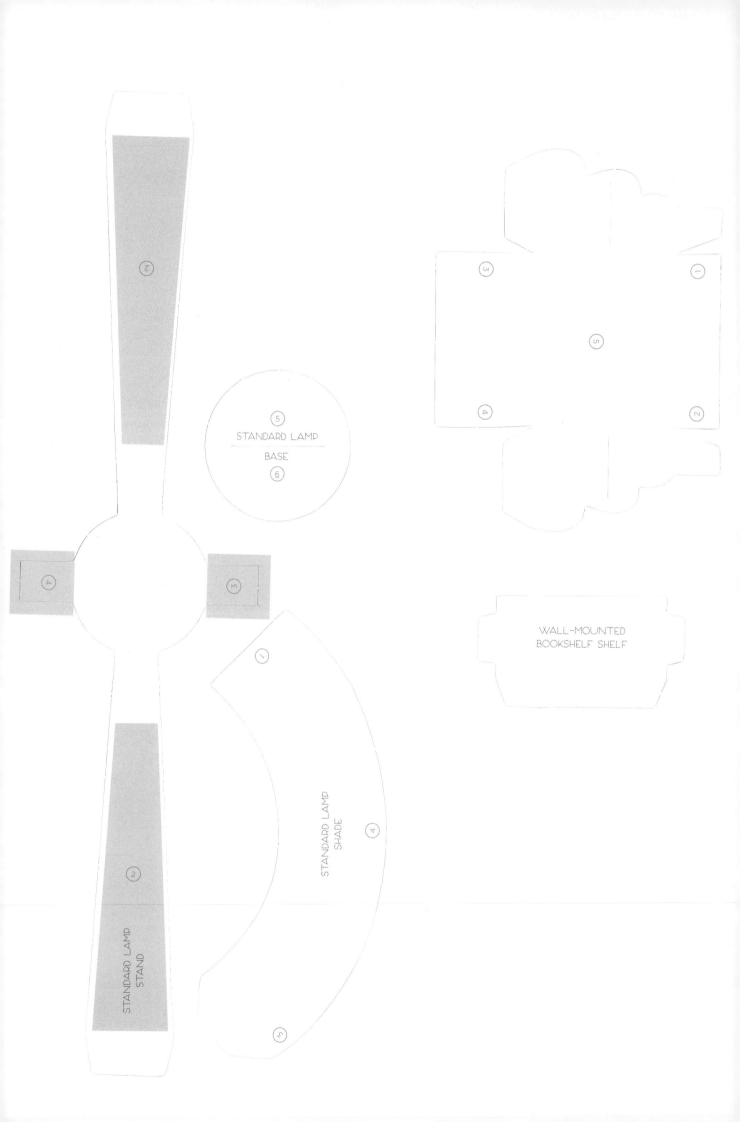

STANDARD LAMP
BASE

STANDARD LAMP
STAND

STANDARD LAMP
SHADE

WALL-MOUNTED
BOOKSHELF SHELF

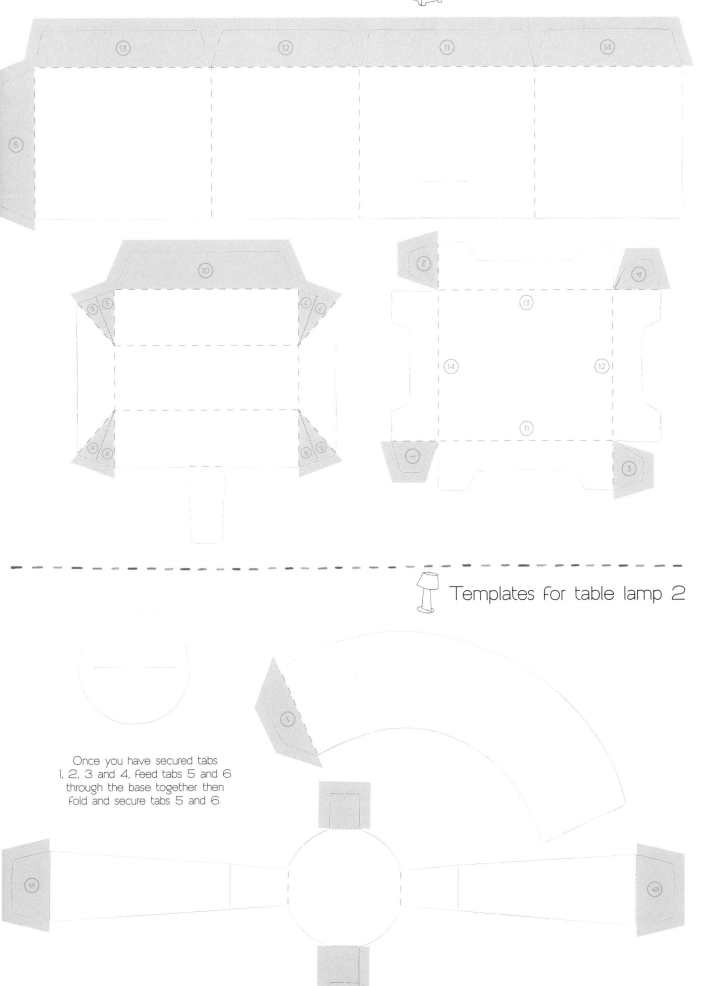

Templates for table lamp 2

Once you have secured tabs
1, 2, 3 and 4, feed tabs 5 and 6
through the base together then
fold and secure tabs 5 and 6.

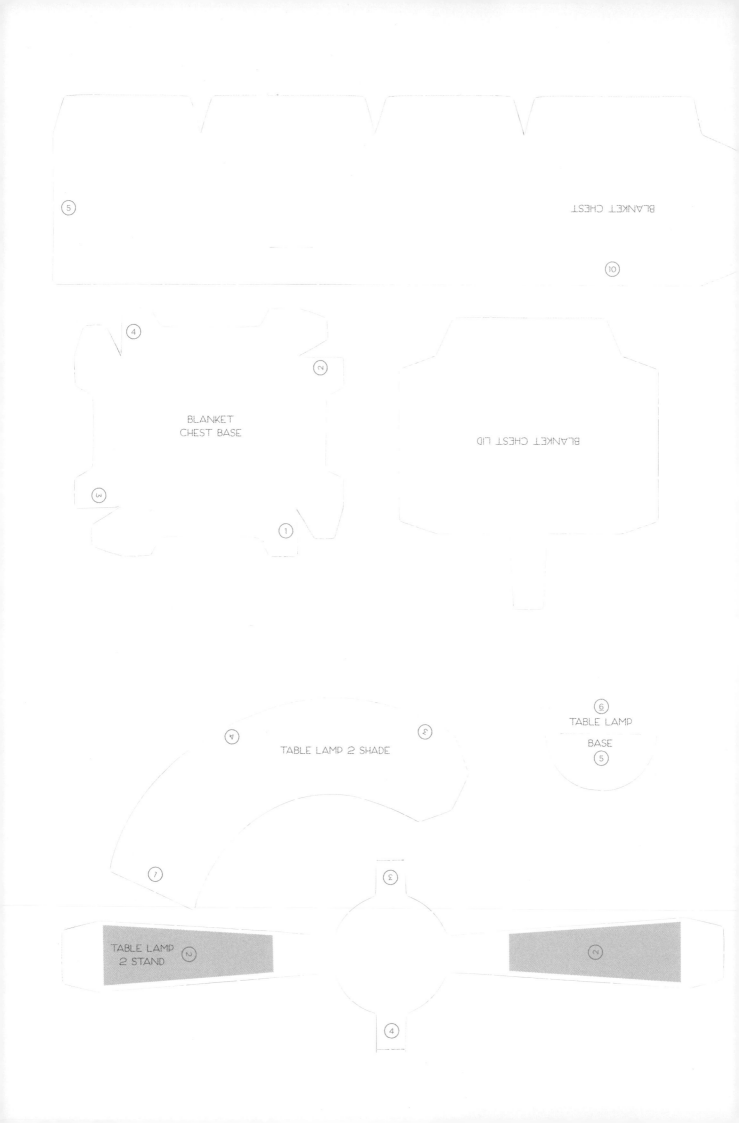

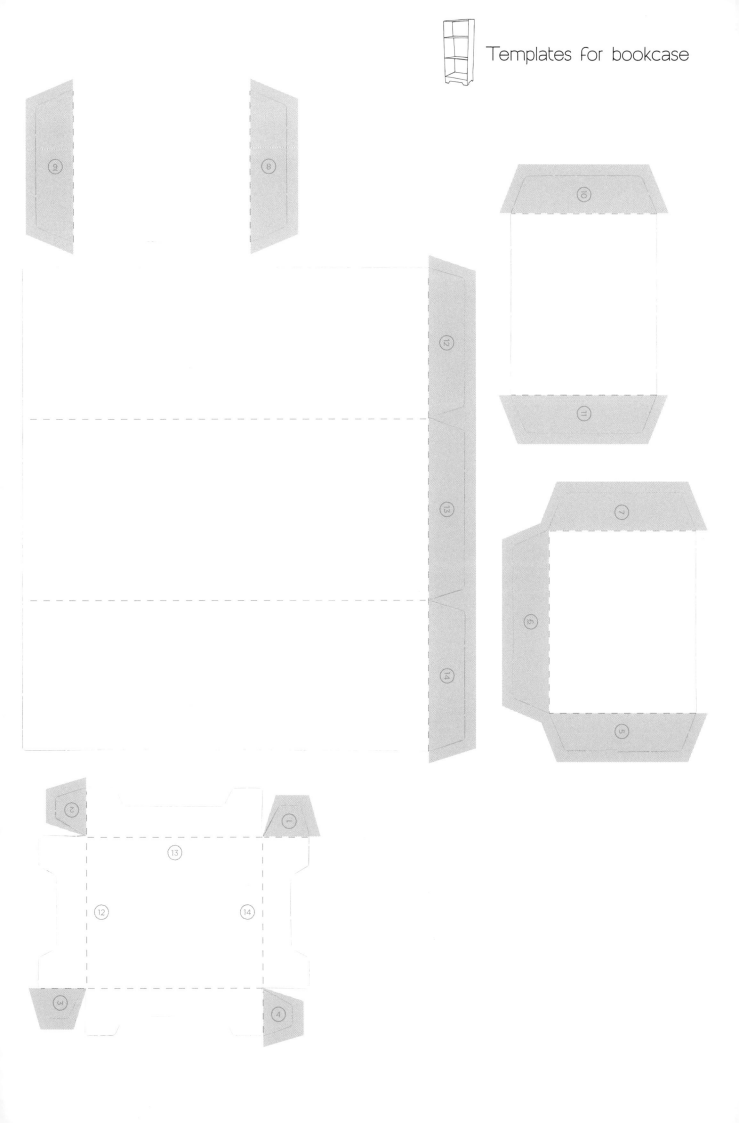

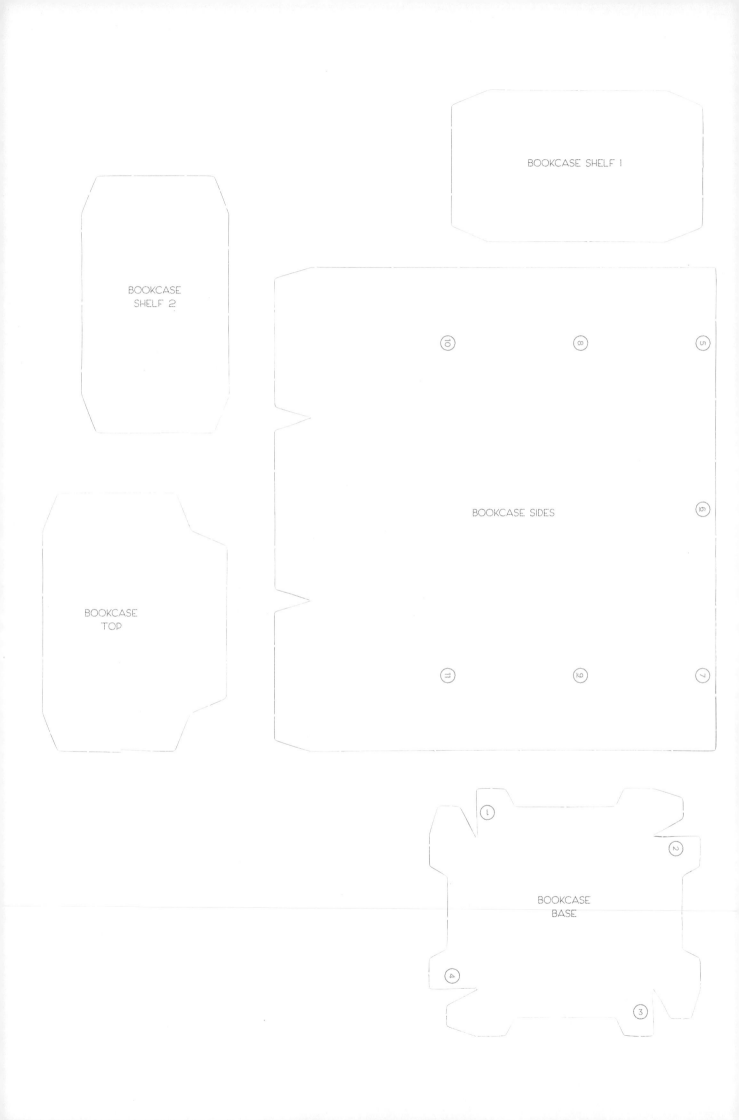

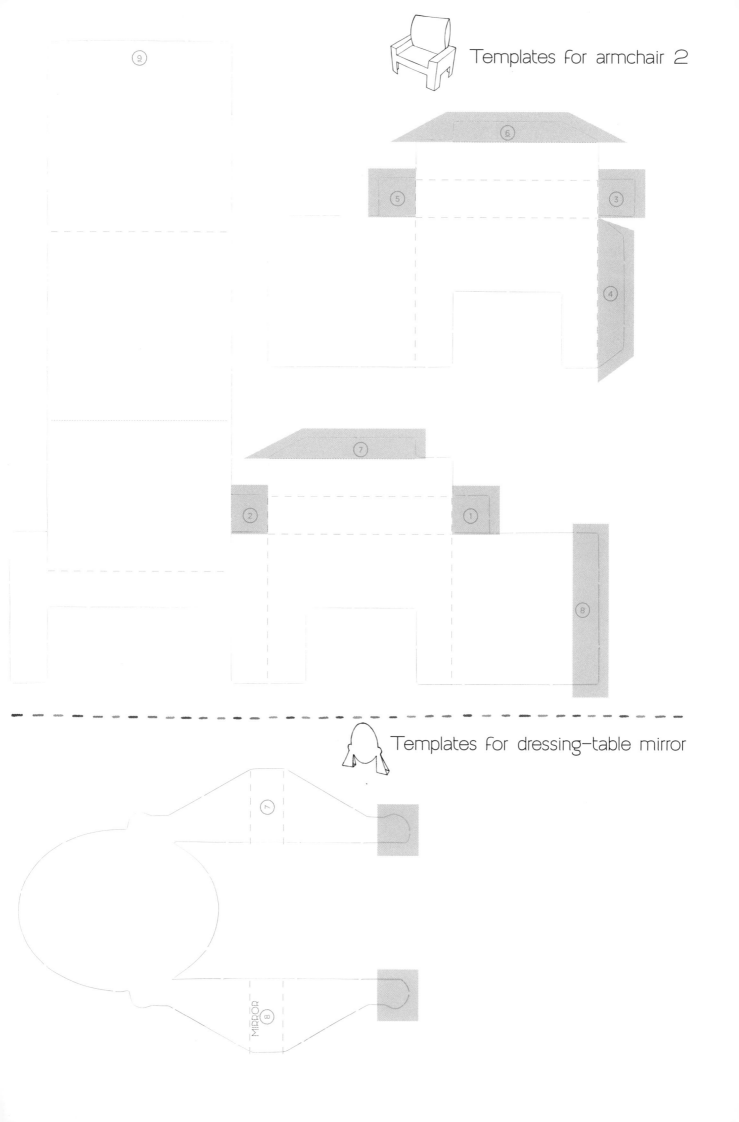

Templates for armchair 2

Templates for dressing-table mirror

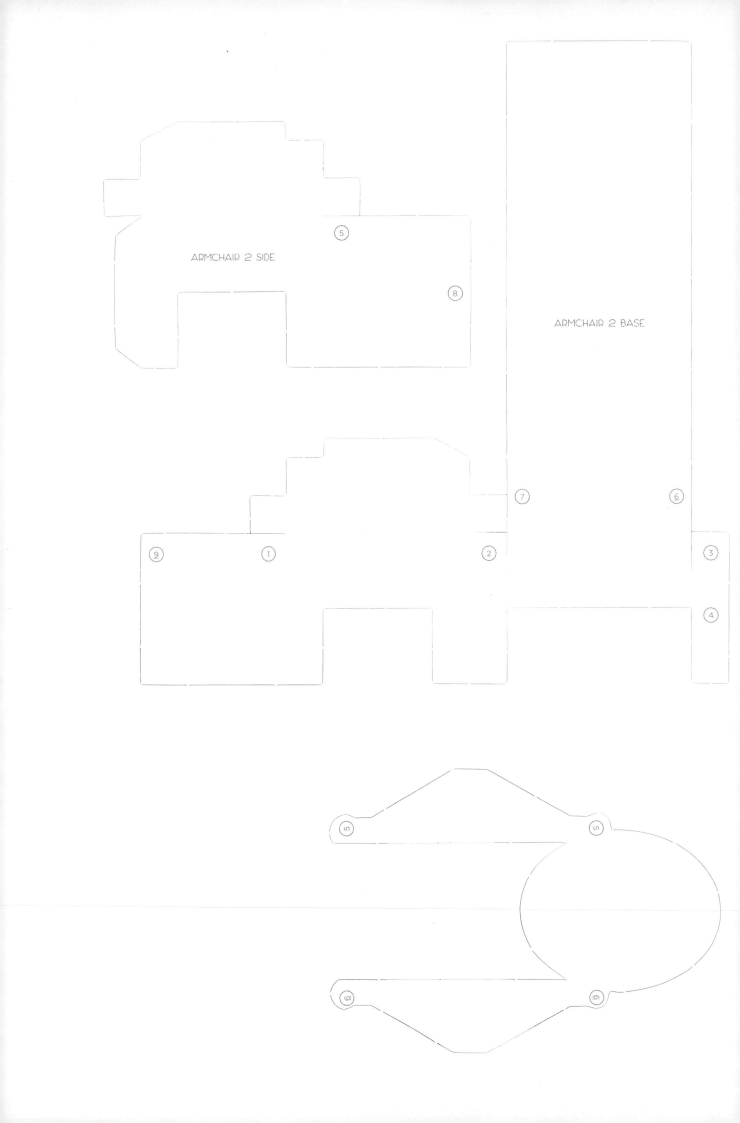

ARMCHAIR 2 SIDE

ARMCHAIR 2 BASE

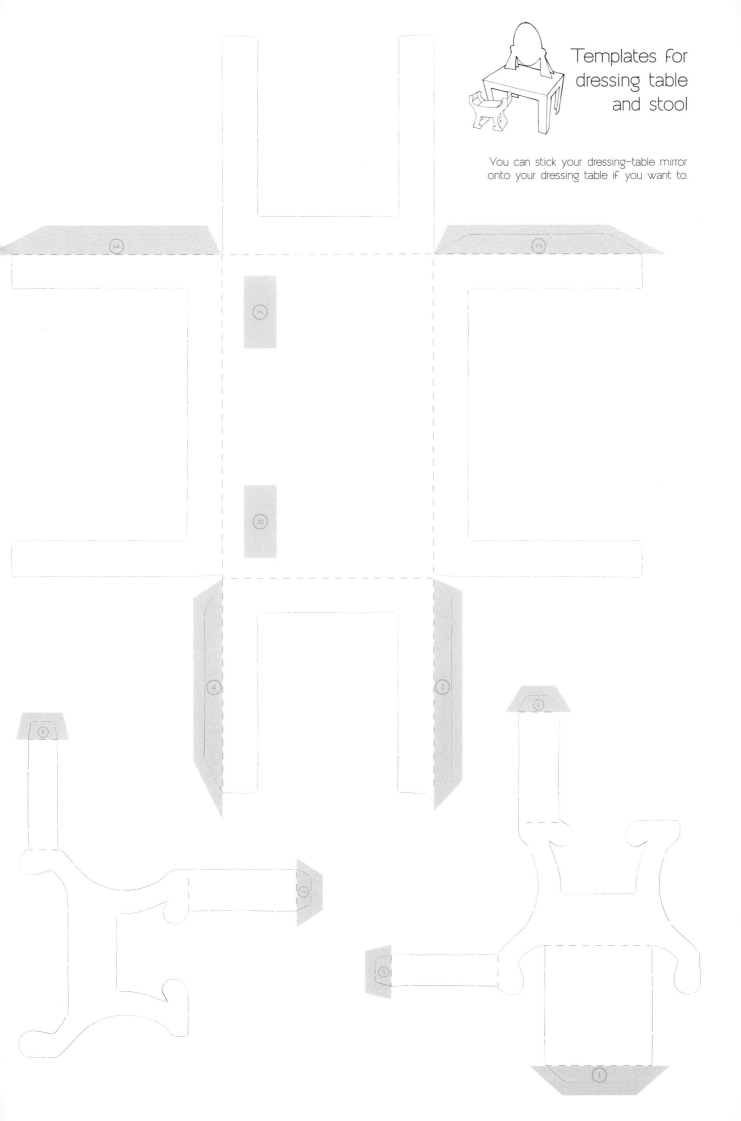

Templates for dressing table and stool

You can stick your dressing-table mirror onto your dressing table if you want to.

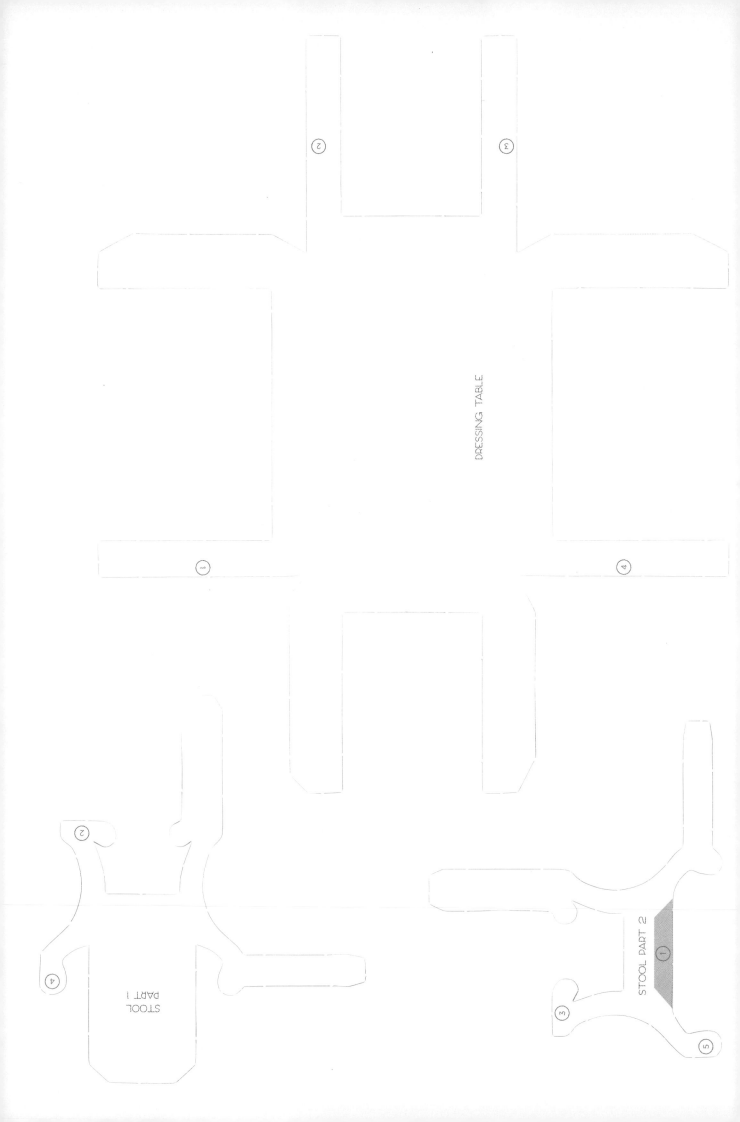

DRESSING TABLE

STOOL PART 1

STOOL PART 2

Press out these pieces of furniture
and see how you can arrange them
on your floor plan on page 19.

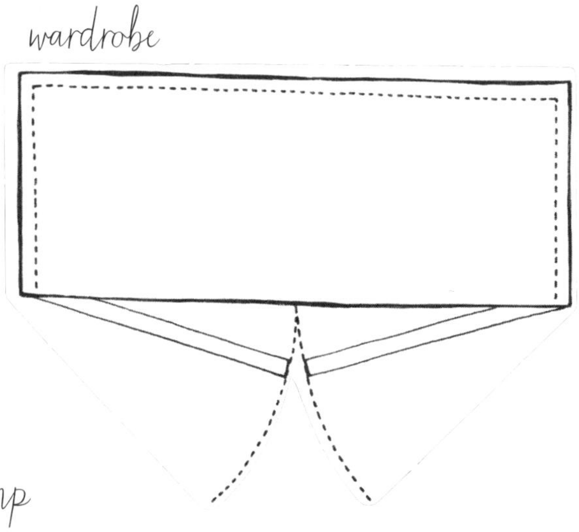

wardrobe

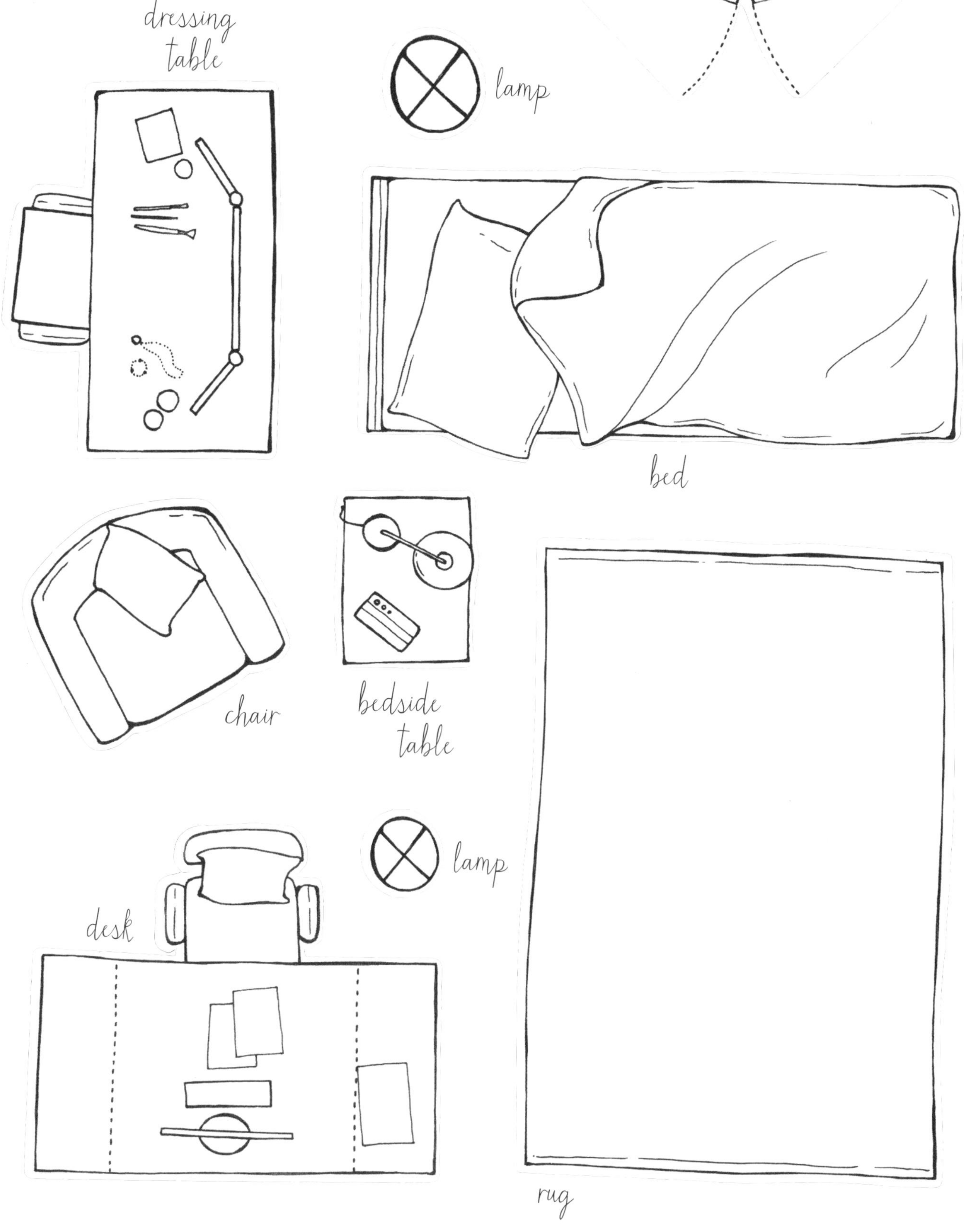

dressing
table

lamp

bed

chair

bedside
table

desk

lamp

rug

Stickers on the other side of the page

Use these stickers to decorate your rooms in rustic and eclectic styles on pages 42 and 43.

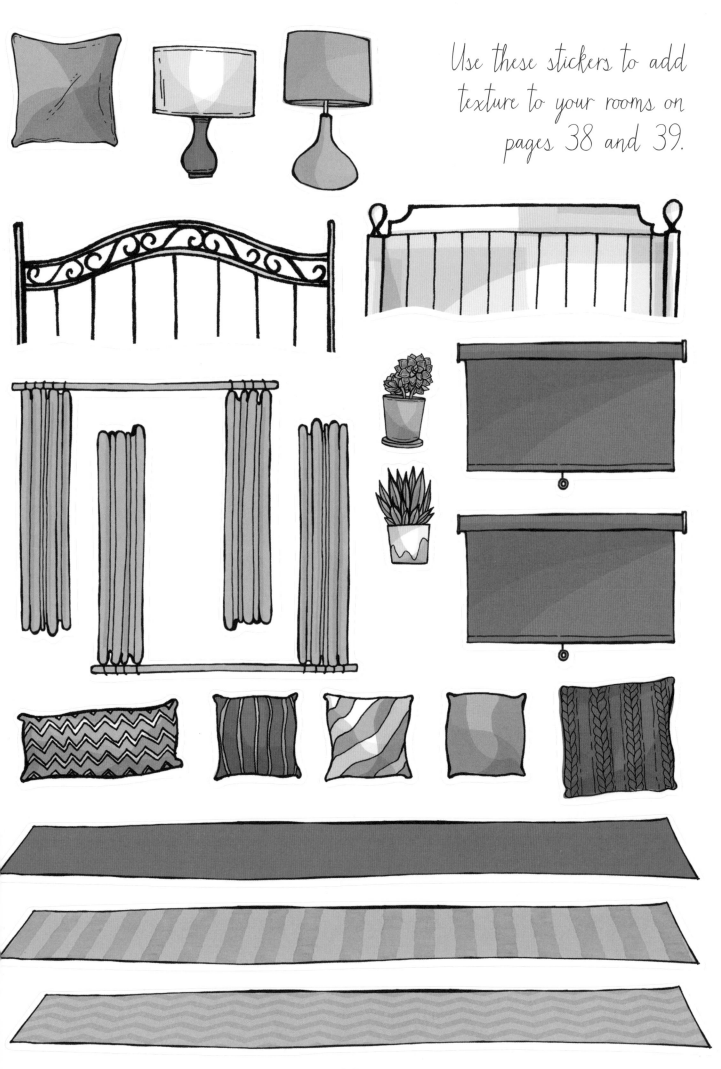

Use these stickers to add texture to your rooms on pages 38 and 39.

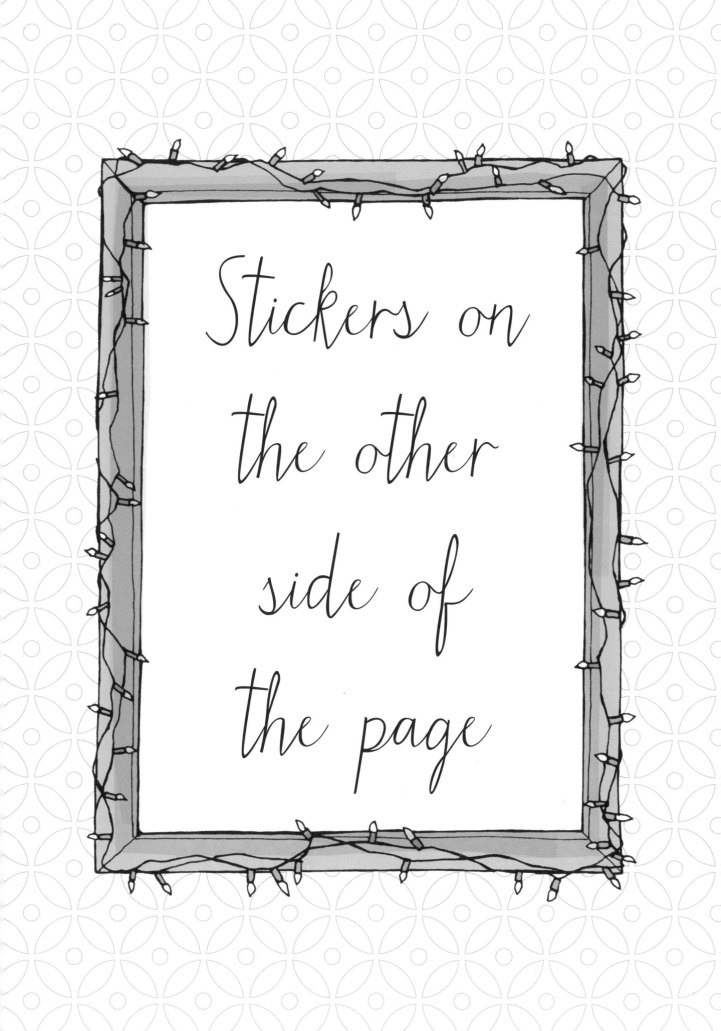

Stickers on the other side of the page

Color in windows and
frames for your room set.

Color in curtains and blinds for your room set.

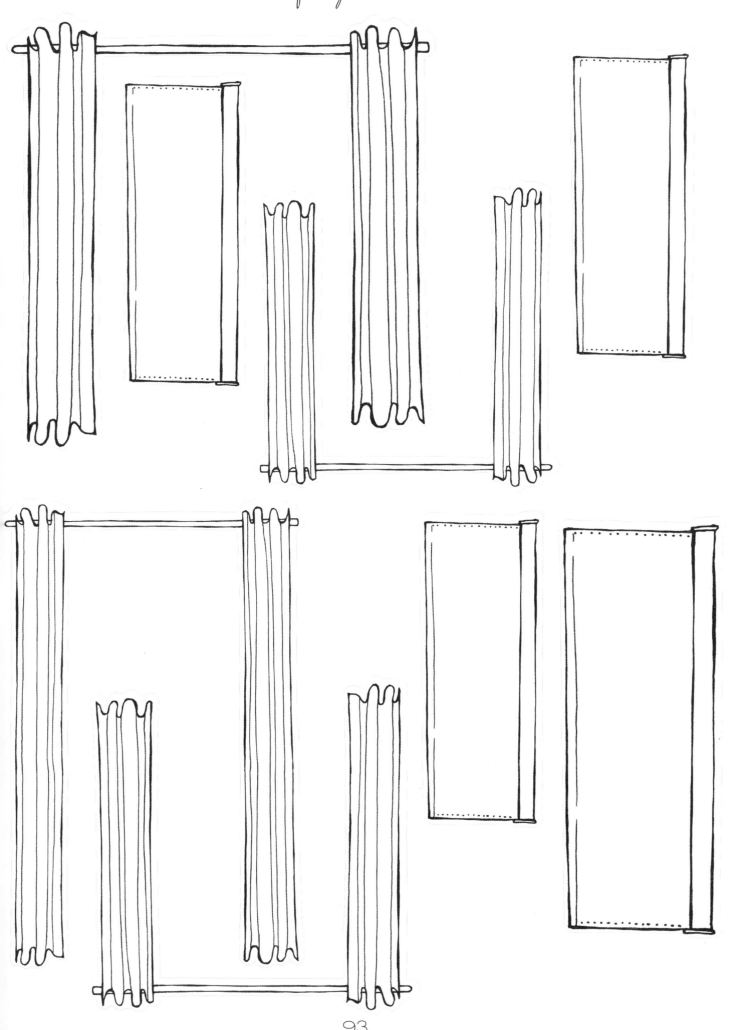

Stickers on the other side of the page

Rugs and cushions
for your room set.